ASSOCIATIVE ECONOMICS

Spiritual Activity for the Common Good

ASSOCIATIVE ECONOMICS

Spiritual Activity for the Common Good

BY

GARY LAMB

Printed with support from the Waldorf Curriculum Fund

Published by:

The Association of Waldorf Schools of North America
Publications Office
65–2 Fern Hill Road
Ghent, NY 12075

Title: *Associative Economics*
Spiritual Activity for the Common Good
Author: Gary Lamb
Editor: David Mitchell
Cover: David Mitchell
Proofreader: Ann Erwin
© 2010 AWSNA
ISBN: 978-1-936367-10-8

Curriculum Series

The Publications Committee of AWSNA is pleased to bring forward this publication as part of our *Curriculum Series*. The thoughts and ideas represented herein are solely those of the author and do not necessarily represent any implied criteria set by AWSNA. It is our intention to stimulate as much writing and thinking as possible about Waldorf education, including diverse views. Please contact us with feedback on this publication as well as requests for future work.

David S. Mitchell
For AWSNA Publications

TABLE OF CONTENTS

Dedication 7

Acknowledgements. 8

Preface: From Experience to Insight 9

PART ONE: Context and Background

Chapter 1
The Nature of This Work. 19

Chapter 2
Rudolf Steiner as Social Reformer and Activist. 23

Chapter 3
Economic Renewal, Cosmology, and the Meaning of Life 29

PART TWO: The Threefold Nature of Social Life
and Associative Economics

Chapter 4
The Threefold Nature of Social Life 35

Chapter 5
The Fundamental Social Law:
A New Foundation for Economic Life. 48

Chapter 6
The Transformation of the Competitive Market and Capitalism:
Building an Associative Economy 62

PART THREE: Aspects of the Threefold Nature of Social Life
and Associative Economics

Chapter 7
Trans-Sector Economic Associations:
Earthly and Spiritual Potentials 77

Chapter 8
Freedom, Funding, and Accountability in Education 86

Chapter 9
The Economic Necessity for
Educational and Cultural Freedom. 93

Chapter 10
Individual and Cultural Freedom 96

Chapter 11
Rights and Single-Payer Systems for
Education and Health Care 99

Chapter 12
Economic Indices and Basic Human Needs 103

Chapter 13
Money and Morality:
From Citizens to Supra-Rulers 106

Chapter 14
True Price 111

Chapter 15
Egoism and Social Life 117

PART FOUR: From Thoughts to Moral Actions

Chapter 16
An Associative Relations Audit as a Means of Transformation 120

Chapter 17
National Leverage Points 128

Chapter 18
Local Leverage Points 133

Chapter 19
Aligning Pedagogy and Finance in a Waldorf School 136

Chapter 20
From Big Thinking and Small Steps to
Systematic Change 143

Endnotes 145

Bibliography. 160

Let no one be only concerned with his own interests:
Let each one strive for the good of the other.
— 1 Corinthians 10

It is given to each and every one to make the working
of the Spirit apparent is his own way, always in a
positive and furthering sense.
— 1 Corinthians 12

Let all that is done among you be done in love.
— 1 Corinthians 16

From the Letters of Saint Paul

Acknowledgements

A number of people have helped in the creation and completion of this book. Judith Soleil and Judith Keily at the Rudolf Steiner Library in Harlemville, NY, provided valuable assistance in obtaining reference materials. I was fortunate to have a number of colleagues who graciously reviewed various chapters as the book progressed. These include John Bloom, Ben Borkovitz, Gregg Davis, Robert Karp, Jan Kibler, Patrice Maynard, Christopher Schaefer, and Jim Willets. Several people provided valuable comments after the initial draft was completed, including Hilary Corsun, Sarah Hearn, Harry Kretz, Jade Lamb, and Marc Clifton. Special thanks go to Sara Ciborski and Sherry Wildfeuer for their editing assistance with the final manuscript.

I also gratefully acknowledge receiving financial support from the Rudolf Steiner Charitable Trust, the Foundation for Rudolf Steiner Books, Inc., Jim Freeman, David Andrew Schwartz, Shawn Sullivan, and Jim Willets.

Finally, I wish to thank the Waldorf Curriculum Fund and the Publications Team from the Association of Waldorf Schools of North America, led by David Mitchell, for the final editing, proofreading, layout, printing, and distribution of this book.

From Experience to Insight

As a general orientation, I will begin by describing some life experiences that have shaped my understanding of social life, including economics, as essentially connected to the spiritual foundations of the human being and the world.

What Do You Do with Sick Money?

In my mid-twenties I went through a brief gambling period. During it I had an experience regarding the nature of money that has stayed with me the rest of my life. It occurred one summer in the 1970s when I was working for a friend refurbishing his two-story garage. My financial goal was to earn enough money to pay for a year of study abroad that was to begin in the autumn.

Other than a few cinder blocks, the garage had no foundation and as a consequence was slowly sinking into the ground, one side faster than the others. My job was to hand-dig underneath the perimeter of the garage about four feet to get below the frost line, create a temporary support system, reinforce the bearing walls, jack up the building as needed until it was reasonably level, and finally build a permanent concrete foundation in the trenches I had dug. The project demanded hard physical labor along with engineering and mechanical ingenuity, and I experienced it as a rewarding challenge.

One evening after work, a relative of my friend invited me to join him at a local gambling establishment. Gambling at the time was for me more of an amusement than a means of winning money. That is, until one evening when he informed me that one of the events was rigged: Did I want, he asked, to make some easy money? This sounded like a novel experience, and in a moment of thoughtlessness I said, "Sure."

As it turned out, these rigged events occurred with regularity, and I found myself in a peculiar situation by summer's end, possessing what was for me a lot of money.

Throughout the summer I had kept my earnings and my winnings in two separate envelopes. I would from time to time take the money out of the envelopes and place it before me in two stacks side by side. Part of me wanted to merge the stacks of $50 and $100 bills and use it all to finance my year abroad. But looking at each pile, visualizing how I had obtained the money, gave me such different feelings that I just couldn't do it.

Two words come to mind now that clearly distinguish the two different feelings: healthy and diseased. I experienced the money earned through my labor and ingenuity as filled with life and potential energy. The money gained through illegal gambling seemed infected with a kind of social disease, and I sensed that whatever I would use the latter for would become infected also. This was not only an intellectual conjecture but a powerful feeling as well.

At summer's end I had to make a decision of whether to merge the two stacks of money. In the end I couldn't do it. But I was in a dilemma. What should I do with the gambling money? Should I give it away to a charity? Burn it? Toss it out of a car window on a crowded street? Take it back and confess my deed, thus exposing a whole ring of people?

There were two issues that I wrestled with. One was that I did not earn the money in any meaningful way. The other was that I had engaged in illegal acts of cheating, if not stealing. I surmised that if the money was simply unearned it could perhaps be redeemed by my giving it to a worthy cause or even by using it for my own education. But the fact that I essentially stole the money made me feel that I had to give it back somehow. And that is what I decided to do.

The last night of the summer I returned with my all the winnings to the place of my ill-gotten gains. I then proceeded to bet and lose my money honestly until it was all gone. Thus was all the money returned to where it had come from, and my conscience relieved. But the real moral of the story for me was the insight that money has different inherent qualities and potentials depending on how it is obtained and how and for what it is used. This was for me an existential reality.

The experiences described in the above story and others that follow are the groundwork for a lifelong involvement in economics. Although I don't consider myself an academic in the traditional sense, I have engaged in a self-directed curriculum of study and observation, along with extensive practical experience in business, agriculture, and education. My path through economics has two parallel tracks: (1) the economics of agriculture and food distribution and (2) freedom and funding of education. As will be shown below, these parallel tracks have continuous crossties connecting them together.

Track One: Domestic and Local Economy, Agriculture, Manufacturing, Retailing, and Distribution

When I was five years old, I had what then was a traumatic experience. My parents, baby sister, and I moved from a rented apartment to our own home on two acres outside of a small village in the Adirondack Mountains in upstate New York. The first time my father took me to visit our new home I left him conversing with the current owners and went out the back door to look around. I then saw something that thrilled me to the core—a backyard baseball field!

At that age and for many years thereafter my favorite activity was playing baseball. Nothing else came close. Now it appeared that I was going to have my own ball field and I was almost dizzy with excitement. I could see the well-worn base paths. It didn't matter that first and second base were rock outcroppings and that there were a couple of poplar trees in right field. As I took all this in, my father came and stood beside me, gazing over the field. I imagined he was having the same vision that I was until he broke the silence and said, "Yep, this field is going to make a mighty fine vegetable garden." I froze in disbelief. I went into denial. He didn't really say that, I told myself. I tried to calm myself with the idea that he must have been expressing a passing thought—surely the benefits of having a ball field would win out over a vegetable garden. Therefore, I decided to forget his comment and not bring up the subject again. But soon after we moved in my father hired a local farmer to plow under the whole field. I remember standing at the edge of the field watching the tractor turn over the sod row after row. My soul was crushed.

Fortunately, my father's vision of how the land should be used was greater than mine. As it turned out, the vegetable garden became an integral part of our household economy, where I learned gardening skills and to work not just for myself but for others as well.

Our domestic economy was supplemented by a couple of fruit trees in our yard. Also, we foraged for wild blueberries, strawberries, and blackberries, which provided tasty treats in the summer. All surplus food was put in the root cellar or canned by my mother. I took up hunting and fishing with my father, which added to our food supply throughout the year. In the Adirondacks in the 1950s and 1960s hunting and fishing were as much matters of livelihood as sport.

When I became legally employable at age 14, I began working on area truck farms as a laborer, utilizing the skills I learned in our home garden. I did this each summer until I was 18 years old. Thus were my early experiences in economy closely related to agriculture and nature.

During these years I was familiar with another type of earth-related economic activity: iron ore mining. The village we lived near was interspersed with mineshafts and ore pits. I remember as a child hearing the rumble and feeling the earth shake when blasting would occur in the mine shafts deep below in earth. I learned later that one of my uncles had died from one of those blasts. From our yard I could see, across the road and through the trees, trains with boxcars laden with crushed ore as they headed to the ore dock on Lake Champlain.

Mining was a main source of employment in the Adirondacks from the mid-1800s until the late 1960s, when most of the mining operations were shut down. I experienced directly the devastating effect of widespread unemployment in a community through my neighbors, uncles, aunts, and cousins.

During the summers of my college years I switched from agricultural work to building and construction in my father's firm. I remember the day I turned 18 when I became old enough to work on construction sites. From one day to the next I went from earning a dollar an hour as a sweat-back farm laborer to three dollars an hour as a construction worker. It felt odd to be suddenly making the same pay as mature men with families to support. Nevertheless I was grateful to be able to earn enough each summer to pay my way through college.

My summers working on various construction projects—a hospital radiation center, a university science building, a chapel, a bank, and a union recreation center—provided me with an insider's perspective of the construction industry. This was informed by my college studies, which included structural design and engineering.

In addition to my work experience as a laborer, mason tender, and apprentice carpenter, I learned about the whole building process from architectural and engineering design to project bidding and construction through my father, who was often the project superintendent where I worked. I could observe the human intelligence that went into the design of the buildings from an engineering and architectural perspective, as well as the wide range of skills of the various tradesmen. I observed the interplay of company owners, management, and workers; the precise timing and coordination of each phase of construction; the labor-saving and hence money-saving capacity of machinery and technology; and management pressures to stay within projected costs.

Following my college years my first significant employment was with Weleda, USA, an anthroposophically-based pharmaceutical and body-care company. I started out as a shipping clerk and worked my way up to toiletry production manager. Here I not only continued my involvement with agriculture by overseeing a biodynamic herb garden but also became involved at various times in processing, quality control, packaging, and distribution of the firm's remedies, body-care products, teas, and elixirs.

Managing this small manufacturing facility, I experienced directly the efficacy of the division of labor and appropriate technology and the human benefits of a team-orientated work environment. I took pricing and efficiency as an ethical responsibility on behalf of both customers and workers and experienced the greatest joy whenever I could increase efficiency without diminishing the high quality of our products or the work environment.

We marketed our products primarily through the natural foods industry, and I frequently attended trade shows around the country, which brought me into constant interaction with other producers, processors, and retailers.

My next position was retail store manager and assistant farm manager at Hawthorne Valley Farm, a diversified biodynamic farm, which has a bakery and a dairy processing facility. The farm distributes its products through farmers markets in New York City, a multiple-site Community Supported Agriculture program, an on-the-farm retail store, and natural food distributors. As the main produce buyer for the farm store, I became friends with many local organic and biodynamic farmers and learned about their personal, professional, and financial struggles. I also interacted with hundreds of store consumers on a daily basis. Thus I gained insight into all aspects of a food economy: production, distribution, and consumption. My biggest questions and struggles during this period concerned how these three aspects of the economy could work together in a cooperative way instead of being in competition with one another, and whether is was possible to be profitable without needing to grow ever larger. It was clear to me and many of my co-workers at the time that organic and biodynamic agriculture could not survive in the conventional market economy based on self-interest and competition. As radical alternatives to conventional agriculture, they require new economic and social forms—including those involving business and land ownership, finance, and consumer relations.

Track Two: Business, Education, and Spiritual Life

In my third year of college I reached an emotional rock bottom. It was in the early 1970s, the Vietnam War was in full swing, there were protest marches in the streets and drug busts on campus. I had been raised in a Christian tradition but my fellow students convinced me through intellectual deftness that there was no God. My courses of study, while profound, appeared to have no inner connection. Marxism, which held no appeal for me, seemed to be the only alternative to exploitative capitalism. My fractured soul was a reflection of a fractured world.

Then a friend suggested I read a book by the anthroposophist Rudolf Steiner. All the titles sounded like the world of religion or spirituality that I had recently rejected as a non-reality. I resisted reading any at first, but eventually ordered one called *Knowledge of Higher Worlds*. The introductory sentences riveted me, beginning with:

> There slumber in every human being faculties by means of which he can acquire for himself a knowledge of higher worlds. …There remains only one question—how to set to work to develop such capacities.[1]

I sensed here religion and spirituality without the dogma, something that would reveal the inner connectedness of the human being and the surrounding world.

At age 26 my obligations to family and country were fulfilled: My mother, whom I had been caring for, had passed away from a brain tumor, and I had completed a two-year conscientious objector duty in a hospital. I decided to work practically with the spiritual insights of anthroposophy. Waldorf education and biodynamic agriculture were among several such possibilities. I opted to train as a Waldorf teacher even though I had never had set foot in a Waldorf school. I visited the Waldorf School of Garden City situated on the campus of Adelphi University, which offered a masters degree in Waldorf education at that time. The secretary of the school gave me a personal tour even though the school was closed for Easter vacation. I saw the children's workbooks and artwork and learned about the curriculum that educated the whole child placing equal emphasis on the capacities of thinking, feeling, and willing; fostered creativity and imagination; and provided for a balance between art and science. I felt deeply the contrast of all this with my own education and the resulting inadequacies. At the end of the tour, she asked me if I would like to join the teacher-training program. I said, "No, I don't feel qualified. I'd rather join the kindergarten!" For me this response was not a joke.

In my early thirties, I became bedridden with pneumonia and was out of work for a month. I remember lying in bed thinking that I could not get up until I found a new motivation in life. I wasn't dissatisfied with what I was doing. It was enjoyable and had meaning and ideals behind it. But something had changed: I felt I needed a new or an additional calling. But what was it? About the only thing I could do in my condition was read. So I began reading books by Rudolf Steiner, at first randomly looking for hints, for something that would speak to me as a message in a passage or a title. Eventually, I started to see a pattern as certain thoughts coalesced around Rudolf Steiner's social threefolding ideas.

I could feel the excitement and energy that come with discovery—the discovering of what I began to see as my life's work. I was sure now that my task had something to do with individual freedom and education, which had something to do with money and business. Money? Education? Freedom? Business? How did these relate? Out of this swirl of thoughts I formed the idea that I should start my own business that would fund an independent school that could be financially accessible to all. It would educate children to be free creative human beings who would change the world of business. I got out of bed, returned to work, and announced my resignation. I was moving on.

Crossties: How the Chapter Contents Emerged

Rudolf Steiner, anthroposophy, and social threefolding in connection to economic and social renewal—these are the key and inspiration for all my social endeavors, including this book. In particular, I have studied and discussed in group contexts the essence and practical applicability of what Rudolf Steiner called the *Fundamental Social Law* and its corollaries in various fields of social life. This Law, as will be elaborated in this book, posits cooperation and care for others as the foundation for a socially responsible associative economy. It is as fundamental to such an economy as the principles of competition and self-interest are to the modern market economy. It is also an ancient spiritual tenet from which all of Steiner's social ideas can be derived.

The content of Chapter 6 on the transformation of the competitive market and capitalism is based on the 12th grade economics courses that I taught at four Waldorf schools over 13 years. Teaching by analogy is a recommended Waldorf method for the high school years. I did so by having the students do a comparative study of socialism, capitalism and the modern market economy, and an associative economy in a threefold social organism. Illustration 2, typical of our coursework, provides such a comparison. During the course we also had another column to take into consideration, the socialist perspective.

Much of the material in Part 3 on education is based on my experiences in the independent Waldorf school movement as a parent, admissions director, development director, and high school teacher. I also drew upon my experiences as the director of the Hope Through Education, a privately funded voucher program that helped families to send their children to private schools, and my experiences as a founding board member of TEACH NYS, a lobby organization that advocates for education tax credits in New York State.

The Associative Relations Audit presented in Chapter 16 emerged from my work with managers at Hawthorne Valley Farm in the effort to find new ways to work more associatively within the organization and with other businesses.

Chapter 1

The Nature of This Work

This book offers a spiritually based sociology that goes beyond the parameters of a traditional treatise on economics. The term *spiritual* refers here to the eternal essence of the human being, of nature, and of the cosmos. It does not necessarily refer to any particular religious belief system. The soul element of the human being is the intermediary or bridge between spiritual essence and the body. This includes the soul functions of thinking, feeling, and willing.

The book is concerned with relationships and community building as much as with factors of production, consumption, labor, and finance. Relationships here include not only our relations to fellow human beings but also to nature and to the divine. Likewise, community building includes any individual or group effort intended to provide something indispensable—product or service—for the body, soul, or spirit of another person or group of people, in a way that expresses respect and gratitude. This characterization can also apply to the production side of an economic life that is imbued with social responsibility.

This book will consider certain hypotheses while appealing to the reader's own inner and outer experiences, common sense, and ideals. These hypotheses are supported by specific examples with enough references to current authors, researchers, and activists to enable readers to find additional information if so desired. From these hypotheses emerge suggestions of how to help implement an associative economy as well as identify the requisite human capacities needed to work within it. One suggestion discussed is a relationship audit for businesses and farming enterprises. The audit helps managers and workers evaluate 13 types of relations within their organizations and between their organization and the surrounding community.

Considering Rudolf Steiner's Social Ideas

This exploration of modern economics, business, and money will draw primarily but not exclusively upon the social ideas of Rudolf Steiner (1861–1925), a European philosopher, social reformer, educator, and esotericist, mainly known today as the founder of Waldorf education, biodynamic agriculture, and anthroposophical medicine.

There are several reasons why Rudolf Steiner's social ideas should be considered when analyzing our current economic system and proposing systemic change. One is that his ideas already influence many leaders in alternative economic and social initiatives and movements. These include community supported agriculture, community land trusts, ethical banking, social finance, local or complementary currencies, sustainable agriculture, green politics, medical and educational freedom, and complementary medicine.[2] Also, his spiritual and social ideas have inspired unique community initiatives such as the worldwide Camphill movement for children and adults with special needs, with over a hundred communities on five continents; life-sharing communities for adults with special needs in Massachusetts, New Hampshire, and several other states; the Fellowship Community in Chestnut Ridge, New York, which offers elder care; and the multifaceted Sekem Community near Cairo, Egypt. In addition, many alternative economic endeavors that are not explicitly linked to Rudolf Steiner are guided by principles that coincide with his ideas, such as the decommodification of land, labor, and capital.

Steiner's social ideas, usually referred to as the threefold social organism or social threefolding (to be explained more fully in Chapter 4), provide a holistic conceptual framework that can be helpful in enabling people from various movements to work together practically. Collaboration of various alternative social movements is vitally important in order to build the force necessary to make fundamental changes in our current economic system and to combat the powerful, entrenched groups that are vested in maintaining the current economic arrangements.

Perhaps the most important reason to bring Steiner's ideas to bear on current social issues is that they take into account the spiritual dimension of the human being, social life, and the natural world. It is becoming apparent that nearly all leaders in the alternative social change movements have a spiritual worldview. Confirming this fact, Robert Karp, Executive Director of the Biodynamic and Farming Association, recently wrote, "Indeed, it is hard to think of a guiding light in the sustainable food and farming movement who [isn't] a profoundly spiritually-minded person." The economist and author David Korten has been expressing a similar thought for years: "I am struck by the fact that nearly every progressive leader of my acquaintance acts from a deep sense of spiritual connection. It is time to give voice to the spiritual foundations of our work through stories that celebrate the unifying spiritual intelligence that is the ground of all being."[3] And Susan Witt, director of the newly formed New Economics Institute, expressed at its founding meeting the need to create a new economic system in terms of spiritual responsibility with the following words: "It is our responsibility—our spiritual task, if you will—to create an economic system that embodies our highest ideals as human beings, one that builds community, advances ecological health, creates beauty, provides sustainability, and encourages mutuality."[4]

Steiner's comprehensive spiritual view of economic and social problems and their solutions extends beyond free market capitalism and socialism, both of which posit economic life as the dominant and determinative social force.

Going Beyond Capitalism and Socialism

The threefold social organism is more than simply a mixture of the best features of capitalism and socialism. It is a new imagination of the nature of economic and social life that takes into consideration the whole human being—body, soul, and spirit.

This new imagination provides for:

- three equally important contrasting yet interweaving and inter-dependent spheres—culture, law, and the economy—rather than an economy superior to and dominating the others;
- self-administration for all three spheres instead of corporate-run states or state-run corporations;
- a fair distribution of wealth rather than an unjust distribution of wealth or reliance on a redistribution of wealth;
- means of production held in trust on behalf of a community and privately managed instead of private- or state-owned and managed;
- true democratic equality in the political realm instead of interest group pluralism;
- efficient, highly personal, non-competitive markets instead of impersonal competitive markets or impersonal state-controlled markets;
- a foundation for moral and social development that resides in individual human freedom rather than in the so-called morality of the market, moral imperatives of the state, or religious or scientific fundamentalism;
- workers as co-producers and partners with management rather than as competitors or as a pawns of the state.

These principles will be explained and elaborated in the following chapters.

Chapter 2

Rudolf Steiner as Social Reformer and Activist

Although his public efforts as a social reformer and activist occurred mainly between 1917 and 1922, the roots of Rudolf Steiner's activism are found in his early philosophical work, *Intuitive Thinking as a Spiritual Path: A Philosophy of Freedom*, first published in German in 1894 when he was 33 years old. In it he addresses the question of free will: "Is a human being spiritually free, or subject to iron necessity of purely natural law?"[5] According to Steiner, attaining free will is a moral process in which a person progresses toward higher and higher states of self-awareness, self-control, and self-directed will. In *Intuitive Thinking* he describes this process as an inner path of development achieved through a rigorous training and refining of individual thinking. The aim of this striving for freedom he calls ethical individualism—an individualism that is permeated with social awareness and responsibility. Thus we can see early in Steiner's work the importance he places on inner transformation and the development of higher-order faculties as a foundation for outer effort on behalf of social renewal.

From 1899 to 1904, Steiner taught at the Berlin Workers College, a school for men and women from the working class, started by Wilhelm Liebknecht, an associate of Karl Marx. Although not a supporter of Marxism, Steiner quickly became one of the most popular teachers at the college. He was eventually forced to leave by the leaders of the college against the wishes of the students. The main factor in his dismissal was his unremitting support of human freedom, which clashed with the school's Marxist ideology.

In 1905 and 1906, Steiner began speaking and writing about the Fundamental Social Law.[6] This law is the foundation of all of his later writings and lectures on economics. He describes it as an ancient spiritual tenet that has the same validity as the laws of nature.[7] One way to characterize the Fundamental Social Law is as follows:

> The more a person works for the benefit of the community, and the more the community is structured to provide for the needs of each individual, the greater the well-being of the whole community will be.

A main corollary to this law is that human suffering caused by social institutions is a result of egoism, and the more people work out of self-interest or egoism, the more poverty, want, and suffering will be introduced into social life somewhere, sometime. This, of course, is in stark contradiction to a central principle of the modern capitalist market economy: The more people work out of self-interest, the more productive they will be and, consequently, the more prosperous society will be as a whole. It is important to note, however, that Steiner's interpretation of the Fundamental Social Law is in no way comparable with traditional interpretations of socialism, as we will see.

While not outwardly active as a social reformer from 1906 to 1917, he did engage in activities that were aimed at strengthening cultural life through the spiritual science he developed, known as Anthroposophy.[8] He created new artistic methods for the visual and performing arts and for architecture. He also gave numerous lectures on a modern spiritual-scientific interpretation of Christianity.

Another important activity during this time period was his study of the human body as an expression of soul and spirit. This led to his insights into the threefold nature of the human organism and, in turn, to an understanding of the threefold nature of the social organism. He maintains that in striving to understand how the human organism consists of the dynamics and interrelations of the three primary systems—nerve-sense, rhythmic, and metabolic—we can develop thinking helpful for understanding the dynamics of social organism.[9]

In 1917, near the end of World War I, Rudolf Steiner was approached by a German diplomat, Otto von Lerchenfeld, who asked him what could be done after the war ended to prevent similar cataclysms in the future. Steiner responded with a description of the inherent threefold nature of social life and the appropriate function and jurisdiction of the three main sectors—economics, culture, and politics—and how they need to relate to each other if there is to be any hope for lasting peace in the world. A small but determined group of people quickly took up these suggestions as a real solution to human exploitation, civil strife, and political warfare. They helped distribute to leading officials in Germany and Austria memoranda written by Steiner describing the main features of a threefold social organism as the foundation for bringing about cultural and social renewal in Central Europe.[10] Although some high ranking officials thought that these innovative ideas had merit, they were too entrenched in old ways of operating politically to take them up for systemic change.

The supporters of social threefolding worked with Steiner on many different fronts. In addition to their political efforts, they formed an association to promote threefold ideas to the public and industry. This operated like a think tank, publishing a journal and sponsoring trained speakers who were versed in social threefolding. Steiner himself gave hundreds of lectures on social threefolding in venues ranging from barrooms and factories to concert halls.[11] He maintained that all three of the main spheres of social life—culture, law, and the economy—were of vital importance, and no one of them should dominate or control the others. One effort to reach the general public was his appeal, "To the German People and the Civilized World." It was endorsed by well-known personalities at the time and inserted in leading newspapers in

Germany in 1919. Also in 1919 he published a book on social threefolding, *Towards Social Renewal*, which became a best seller in Germany.[12]

In 1920 Steiner helped set up two corporations, Futurum Konzern AG in Switzerland and Der Kommende Tag (The Coming Day: A Shareholder Corporation for Furthering Economic and Spiritual Values) in Germany. They were meant to be organizational forms for generating revenue for cultural initiatives such as schools and research laboratories.

By 1922 most efforts by Steiner and his colleagues ceased to publicly promote social threefolding. As the World War receded into the background, hyperinflation in Germany, misapprehension by labor union officials, and the tendency to revert to old thought habits all contributed to the relatively short-lived interest in Steiner's social ideas outside the circle of people who valued his insights in other areas.

Nevertheless, there still exist today important initiatives founded during that time period as part of the threefold efforts. One example is the Waldorf school movement. In 1919, Emil Molt, an industrialist and enthusiastic supporter of Rudolf Steiner's social ideas, asked Steiner to help him start a school for the children of the workers of the Waldorf Astoria cigarette factory in Stuttgart, Germany, which he managed. The School was part of the *Coming Day* experiment and received significant financial support through it. Molt envisaged the Waldorf School as an example of an independent cultural endeavor that would spearhead the elevation of cultural life and the liberation of education from state control. Molt's and Steiner's aim was to establish an independent school as free as possible from onerous state regulations, which was accessible to families regardless of their financial circumstances.[13] There are now over a thousand Waldorf or Rudolf Steiner schools worldwide. Another important business that was part of the Futurum AG that still exists today is the Weleda AG, a private corporation based in Switzerland and global manufacturer of cosmetics and natural remedies with annual sales of over $300 million.

In 1922, within a few weeks of each other, Steiner made two other noteworthy efforts to expound his social ideas. The first was a series of 14 lectures given in Switzerland on the fundamentals of economics.[14] Instead of addressing social issues from the macro social level of a threefold social organism, he focused on the economic sphere to an audience comprised mainly of economic students. In these lectures he expanded his thoughts on the Fundamental Social Law and social threefolding. He also characterized the economy as a self-enclosed world system; distinguished the differing natures of loan, purchase, and gift money; and elucidated the benefits of replacing an impersonal market with a market coordinated by producer, distributor, and consumer associations. We will look more closely at these themes in upcoming chapters.

The other effort, in Britain, was a series of talks at a conference titled "Spiritual Values in Education and Social Life" at Manchester College, Oxford.[15] In these he stated that his book *Towards Social Renewal*, which had been a best seller in Germany, was now almost forgotten because hyperinflation had thwarted most efforts to implement social threefolding ideas. Even so, he felt people in the Western world could benefit greatly from the implementation of social threefolding ideals. Interestingly, relatively soon afterward favorable reviews of the English translation of *Towards Social Renewal* began to appear in the United States and Britain. An economist in a 1923 *New York Times* book review praised it as "the most original contribution in a generation" to sociological literature. The reviewer went on to say:

> The author ... has addressed himself to social problems from an unusual point of view, producing the highly interesting conception of the Threefold Commonwealth. ...Most of our books on social maladjustment and the future of civilization are based on either economic or psychological interpretation; Dr. Steiner has what may be called a spiritual interpretation and he would reorganize society in such a way as to bring it into conformity with spiritual realities.[16]

In the same year, a Christian theologian, W.F. Lofthouse, who attended Steiner's lectures at Oxford, wrote a review of Steiner's writings in *The London Quarterly Review*. Like the American economist just quoted, Lofthouse praised his spiritual perspective on social problems:

> An outsider, strolling into the Oxford lecture room last August …might not have suspected that he was listening to the author of [*Towards Social Renewal*], perhaps the most widely-read of all books on politics appearing since the war …
>
> He has offers and hopes for all sides of life. … Steiner has a definite system of ideas and an array of positive aims, clear, synthetic (as he would say) and spiritual. …
>
> And yet he is interested, not in many things, but one. 'Synthesis' is his watchword. Every demand and, still more, every response is to be correlated with every other. A comprehensive view of the world and of man is what the times require, a principle to be applied to all personal and social activities. If this can be found, it will be possible to produce a definite social program, both political and religious.[17]

Steiner never relinquished his insistence on the importance of social threefolding even though it was not taken up in any significant way during his lifetime. Shortly before his death in 1925, he stated that all initiatives that are a part of the Anthroposophical Society, which fosters the spiritual-scientific worldview that he developed, should strive to promote social threefolding even if the rest of the world was rejecting it.[18]

All public efforts in the direction of a threefold social organism had to cease in Germany around 1935 and throughout World War II because the National Socialists considered it a threat to their nationalist views and aims. It wasn't until the 1970s and 1980s that diverse alternative movements in various locations began to take up threefold ideas with significant albeit local impact.

Chapter 3

Economic Renewal, Cosmology, and the Meaning of Life

Our world, so we see and hear on all sides, is drowning in materialism, commercialism, consumerism. ...The root of materialism is a poverty of ideas about the inner and outer world. ... Materialism is a disease of the mind starved for ideas.[19]

> – Jacob Needleman, *The American Soul:*
> *Recovering the Wisdom of the Founders*

Strange as it may sound, we can't just focus on economics to change economic systems. We have to go deeper and further.[20]

> – Riane Eisler, *The Real Wealth of Nations:*
> *Creating a Caring Economics*

First of all, get a broom and out with everything that negates the spirit in economic life. On that depends the future welfare of mankind. ...Away with everything that rejects the spirit in economic life. ... Otherwise, economic chaos will result and with it the general chaos of civilization.[21]

> – Rudolf Steiner, *Spiritual Science as a*
> *Foundation for Social Forms*

All social institutions are an expression of what we think and feel about the world and our fellow human beings, whether we are conscious of it or not. Our thoughts and feelings, in turn, are a reflection of our worldview, which includes our views on the nature of the human being, the meaning and purpose of life, and our core beliefs and values.

The modern market economy, as an example, is both a byproduct and a reinforcement of the materialistic worldview that has gripped human consciousness in recent centuries. Materialism is a perspective that recognizes physical sense-perceptible matter as the only reality and asserts that everything, including thinking, feeling, and willing can be explained in terms of matter and physical phenomena. It is a view that denies the reality of spirit in the human being and nature. Irrefutably, the so-called natural science that is based on materialistic assumptions has with the aid of technology helped make possible great advances in science, medicine, transportation, communication, and many other fields, for which we can be exceedingly grateful. But through the influence of materialism and economic life, our thought power and human ingenuity, which are spiritual capacities, have been employed largely in the pursuit of the limited goals of outer advancement and material rewards. Alan Greenspan, the former Chairman of the Federal Reserve Bank, expressed it this way in his testimony before a House of Representatives Banking Committee in 2002: "It is not that humans have become any more greedy [sic] than in generations past. It is that the avenues to express greed [have] grown so enormously." And we should note that the monetary incentives for expressing greed have also grown enormously.[22]

Given this situation, people within the modern alternative economic movement have come to the highly significant realization that it will not suffice simply to change outer economic structures. As the quotation by Riane Eisler suggests, we need to go much "deeper and further" in order to transform economic life in any meaningful way.[23] For our consideration here, "deeper" means right down to the meaning and purpose of life and the origin of the universe, and "further" means into other fields of social science such as anthropology and sociology, and into the realms of culture and politics. The recognition that we need a worldview that can help us overcome unrestrained egoism in economic life has led alternative economists and businesspeople to search for a more meaningful and comprehensive cosmology or cosmic story than is provided by materialistic natural science. The economist David Korten explains the social effect of materialistic science in this way:

> As [materialistic] science tells the cosmic story, consciousness is nothing more than an illusion born of chemical reactions. It is a story without meaning or purpose that leaves us with little reason to restrain our hedonistic impulses.[24]

Not only does a materialistic worldview offer little incentive to overcome self-interest and greed when opportunities to do so arise, it also provides little or no appreciation of the kingdoms of nature. It persuades us to view the environment abstractly, as merely a natural resource to be exploited for the satisfaction of material needs instead of a source of material and spiritual nourishment that needs to be treated with reverence.

Unlike a materialist perspective, the anthroposophical spiritual science pioneered by Rudolf Steiner provides a spiritually meaningful and powerful cosmic story.[25] It has the potential to help us acquire the insights and courage needed to combat the unrestrained greed and gross inequities that are so common in economic life today, to build a new economy based on care and concern for others, and to acknowledge the underlying unity of human beings and nature.[26]

From the perspective of spiritual science, the physical or material world as we know it is the result of a spirit-to-matter condensation process that occurred over great eons of time.[27] All that we associate today with the material world—the laws of biology, chemistry, physics, and astronomy; and all social groupings, including corporations, political parties, religions, and families—are expressions and manifestations of spirit.

Spiritual science does not contradict or deny the valid findings of natural scientific research, but rather supplements them and makes them more complete. What we can call the spiritual world consists of beings, forces, and laws of which the physical world is a manifestation. And just as we can gain an understanding of the material world through study and research, we can likewise study the indications of spiritual science and conduct spiritual-scientific research into the same phenomena. As with natural science we can use spiritual science to support social life in ways, for example, through education, agriculture, and religion. Waldorf education, biodynamic agriculture, and the Christian Community Movement for Religious Renewal exemplify thriving practical initiatives in these fields that enjoy the benefit of spiritual insight into the human being and nature.[28] Similarly, Steiner used spiritual insight to establish a new foundation for social life, including economics.

An essential component of the spiritual-scientific (anthroposophical) worldview is the evolution of human consciousness. Only when we recognize that human consciousness was once quite different from human consciousness today can we properly evaluate societies and social structures of former and current times.

If we go back in time far enough, we find an innate spirituality as part of the consciousness of all peoples, somewhat similar to the consciousness of indigenous peoples of only a few hundred years ago.[29] Human beings in those earlier times perceived spirit in nature. Consciousness for them was an experience of participation and oneness with nature and with each other. With ever-deeper research into and mastery of the material world and the development of technology—a kind of sub-nature—we have come to experience an increasing separateness from our spiritual heritage. Modern consciousness has enabled us to gain mastery over the physical world but has brought with it a consequent loss of spirit-experience.

The emergence of individual self-consciousness is an important result of this descent into matter. This enhanced sense of individuality is reflected historically in the demand for democracy or political equality.[30] From a spiritual-scientific perspective, the development of natural science, technology, and commerce, with the attendant loss of connection to spiritual realities, is an appropriate and necessary step in the evolution of human consciousness, at least up to a certain point. However, through the course of human evolution, we are meant to reawaken to the objective reality of spirit, but now in full consciousness. The loss of instinctive, innate (automatic) spirituality has made individual freedom a possibility, and has allowed us to develop a strengthened "I" consciousness through which we can and should become conscious co-creators of future human evolution.

However, the advancement toward freedom does not guarantee that we will always make appropriate decisions and choices; freedom also means having the opportunity to become distracted from what is important in life, to be led astray, and to make errors in judgment. We now have crucial decisions to make regarding our social life and the environment. The question is: Can we take the necessary actions soon enough to avert global economic, political, and environmental disasters?

Another important outcome of the evolution of consciousness is the arising of both social and antisocial forces in the human soul. Individualism, and consequently egoism, will grow significantly in the future as human beings progress on the path toward freedom and renewed spirituality.

We cannot eradicate antisocial forces in our souls since they are a natural corollary of growing individualism, self-awareness, and self-actualization. But we can choose to focus our efforts on nurturing and strengthening truly healthy social forces within our being with practices and forms that will be discussed in later chapters.

Steiner describes what he calls an archetypal social phenomenon that takes place in every human encounter. Whenever two or more people communicate there are two polar tendencies at work. One is a social disposition: the tendency to diminish one's self-concerns and thoughts and rather live into the thoughts of the others. The other inclination is the antisocial tendency to remain awake exclusively to one's own thoughts and opinions.

For the most part, there is a continual subconscious oscillation in every human exchange between self-focused attention and attentiveness to the thoughts of others. Since antisocial forces are growing ever stronger, we need to make a continual effort to counterbalance them by developing a greater interest in the thoughts and feelings of others, even if they differ from our own. Rudolf Steiner calls the development of ever more interest in others the foundation or backbone of social life in the future.

In the next section we consider some of the outer arrangements recommended by Steiner that will foster the development of social forces in the human being.

Chapter 4

The Threefold Nature of Social Life

We as a global society are confronted with three root questions.
I find these root questions alive in the hearts and minds of people
across various cultures and civilizations. They are:

1. How can we create a more equitable global economy that would
   serve the needs of all, including today's have-nots and future
   generations?
2. How can we deepen democracy and evolve our political
   institutions so that all people can increasingly directly participate
   in the decision-making processes that shape their context and
   future?
3. How can we renew our culture so that every human being is
   considered a carrier of a sacred project—the journey of becoming
   one's authentic self?[31]

   – C. Otto Scharmer, *Theory U*

The cultural principles of Earth Community affirm the spiritual
unity and interconnectedness of Creation. ...The economic principles
of Earth Community affirm the basic right of every person to a means
of livelihood and responsibility of each person to live in a balanced
relationship with their place on Earth without expropriating the
resources of others. ...The political principles of Earth Community
affirm the inherent worth and potential of all individuals and their
right to a voice in the decisions that shape their lives, thereby favoring
inclusive citizen engagement, cooperative problem solving, and
restorative justice.[32]

– David Korten, *The Great Turning:
From Empire to Earth Community*

As noted in Chapter 2, Rudolf Steiner's work with social threefolding ideas began at the close of World War I in Germany. He was one of the first sociologists to speak of a three-part society—or a threefold social organism, as he called it—consisting of three relatively autonomous, yet interdependent realms: culture, rights, and economics. Intimations of this threefold nature of society can be found in the 18th century slogan of the French Revolution: *Liberty, Egalité, Fraternité*. It is now quite common to find politicians, economists, and sociologists speaking about a three-part society. The quotes above by C. Otto Scharmer, the well-known lecturer at MIT and organizational consultant, and David Korten, a prominent author in the field of alternative economics, attest to this fact.

The question for the future is not so much whether society is threefold but what form of threefold society humanity will bring. The current reality is a three-sectored world order with financial interests and economic life represented by a very limited number of powerful people dominating politics and cultural life. In contrast, both Scharmer and Korten suggest a more balanced threefolding that honors the freedom and rights of all people and the importance of all three aspects of society, which is consistent with Steiner's perspective.[33]

It is important to understand that for Steiner social threefolding is not an outer structure or world order to be imposed onto people and institutions; rather, threefolding is inherent in the nature of social life. It is a formative element that is trying to emerge out of social life itself. Through conscious effort this inner nature now needs to find expression in our social structures and systems in ways that are appropriate and socially healthy in the various regions of the earth.

The Threefold Human Being

As we have seen, before Rudolf Steiner introduced his ideas on the threefold social organism and what has come to be known as associative economics, he spent decades of study and research focused on the nature of the human being, including the interrelation of body, soul, and spirit. It was only after he gained a comprehensive understanding of these complexities that he felt ready to speak about social life. Steiner maintained that this understanding is essential because our outer social structures need to reflect our essence as human beings and our relation to the world. Understanding the human being as a spiritually-imbued living organism can help us to think in a new way about society as a spiritually-imbued social organism.[34]

Steiner describes that physiologically there are three main systems of contrasting activity in the human body: a nerve-sense system centered in the head region, a rhythmic system centered in the mid-region, and the metabolic limb system centered mainly in the lower region and extremities of the body.[35] These three physiological systems that are centered in specific bodily regions nevertheless extend throughout the whole human organism, intertwining and interacting with each other. The proper functioning of each system is dependent on the health and vitality of the other systems and how well they relate to each other. If one system becomes overactive in an area where it should not, illness can arise. For example, when the metabolism works too strongly in the head region, congestion can occur. Or, if nerve sense activity becomes too strong in the metabolism, ulcers can arise.

With the image of the threefold human being as a background, we will now consider some of the main features of a threefold social organism as expressed by Rudolf Steiner.

The Threefold Social Organism:
Balancing Autonomy and Interdependence

The three spheres of culture, rights, and economy can be viewed as three distinct areas of activity that reach out and interpenetrate throughout the whole social organism. Social illness can arise in a manner similar to illness in the human organism; for instance, when powerful economic interest groups dominate our rights, democracy is undermined and becomes diseased. Or, when the political state intrudes on personal liberty, our cultural life becomes impotent.

It is helpful to depict the threefold social organism as three intersecting circles, each representing one of the three main realms of society (see Illustration 1). A simplified image of what in reality is an exceedingly complex living organism, it nonetheless provides a useful starting point for understanding the threefold nature of social life.

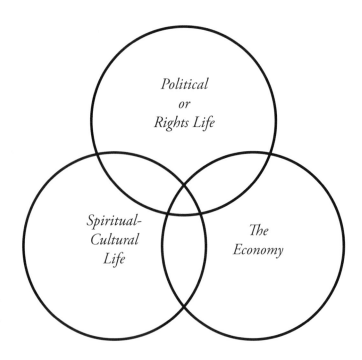

Illustration 1–The Three Spheres of a Threefold Social Organism

Each of these realms is essential for a healthy social life. Like the three physiological systems in the human body, each has distinct yet interdependent functions. Consistent with this perspective, each realm needs to have its own independent administration and governing bodies, and none should dominate or intrude on the others in an inappropriate way. Unfortunately, today, economic interests and economic thinking dominate both the political and cultural realms, including education, and are a primary cause of much of the exploitation and injustice that occurs in the world.[36]

It is essential for the future development of a healthy social life that each sphere be enabled to fulfill its vital function. The function of the spiritual-cultural life, which includes education in the broadest sense, is to foster the full development of each human being, from outer practical skills to the highest moral and social virtues. It follows from this fact that an independent cultural life needs to be based on individual freedom. The function of a healthy political or rights sphere is to foster human relations by recognizing and upholding human rights and maintaining safety and security. Its foundation therefore should be democracy and equality. And finally, the function of the economy from a threefold perspective is to provide for the earthly and spiritual needs of human beings.[37] Its proper basis is altruism or concern for others and society as a whole.

This characterization of the three realms not only represents Steiner's thinking but also is an image of what we can see arising through the efforts of many alternative economic and social justice movements around the world, as is explained in later chapters.[38]

We will now consider briefly each of the three sectors, and how they need to relate to each other in order to achieve maximum social health.

Spiritual-Cultural Life

The primary purpose of the spiritual or cultural realm is to foster to the greatest possible extent the development of the innate capacities that each person brings into earthly life. This will ultimately lead to an understanding of the meaning and purpose of life and our relation to nature and the world.

This development comprises everything from intellectual abilities, artistic capacities, and moral qualities to practical job skills. Education in the broadest sense, including the fields of science, art, and religion, is the primary arena of cultural life. From a spiritual perspective, the highest goals for these fields, respectively, are scientific truth, artistic beauty, and moral goodness. The possibility for world peace depends on the development of these three virtues to the greatest possible degree within each human being and on the degree to which these virtues are able to influence economic and political life.

If we take seriously and do not just give lip service to our recognition of a unique spiritual essence in every individual, then we must ensure that society fosters activities and institutions wherein this aspect of the human being can develop out of its own spiritual nature and laws—not the nature and laws that apply to business and political life. These activities and institutions would include schools, places of worship, care facilities, research labs, theatres, art galleries, festival celebrations, family homes—in short, any educational, cultural, or social activity intended to manifest human creativity or self-expression.

Such institutions and activities cannot fulfill their unique function of enabling the development of spiritual potential if they are directed primarily by political or economic interests and thinking. These have validity in their own realms, but must not be the primary shapers of cultural life.

Thus, an authentic independent cultural life will have much to offer for the growth of a healthy economic and political life: moral strength and social understanding; artistic sensitivity and imaginative creativity; and practical skills and love of meaningful work. It is only through individuals with fully developed creative capacities, vitality, and a strong sense of fellowship that rejuvenating spiritual forces can enter into social life as a whole. These are also the very forces that can counterbalance the socially destructive nature of an economic life devoid of ethical impulses.

Individuals are of little service to themselves or to the world if they do not strive to develop their latent capacities. In this sense, self-interest and individualism are legitimate starting points for spiritual-cultural life. However, the demand for ever greater individual freedom in social life needs to be balanced by a growing sense of responsibility for the welfare of others and tolerance for other people's perspectives. In going beyond personal desires and needs to include the needs of others, we can avoid one-sided individualism and irresponsible behavior. In an independent spiritual-cultural sphere free from coercive economic and political interests, social awareness and responsibility can be added to the initial egoistic motivation for self-development.

How one goes about his or her personal development and education should be the free decision of each adult or the concern of parents or guardians on behalf of their children until they reach adulthood. Freedom and self-determination are the essential principles of a healthy spiritual-cultural life. This includes personal decisions concerning education, religion, nutrition, and medicine.

Steiner maintains that not only self-interest but also competition can appropriately operate in the spiritual-cultural aspect of life. For example, a provider of any type of cultural service—a teacher, for instance—needs to "compete" or win the appreciation of potential families who might send their children to the school where the teacher is engaged. The social conditions necessary for such healthy competition in the cultural realm, including the fields of education, health care, and religion, are individual and professional freedom of thought, freedom of choice, opportunity to be fully informed, and sufficient financial resources on the part of patrons and consumers to access their choices.

With regard to the three soul functions—thinking, feeling, and willing—Steiner suggests that the starting point in the spiritual-cultural development in modern culture is thinking. We need to expand and deepen our normally abstract thinking and our understanding of others in order to enhance and refine our feelings and purposefully direct our will.

In summary, the main function of the spiritual-cultural realm in a healthy threefold social organism is to enable the full development of each individual's capacities.

An authentic cultural life is:

- comprised of education in the broadest sense, including science, art, and religion;
- based on individual freedom, including freedom of thought, choice, expression, and association;
- related initially to self-interested behavior, the soul function of thinking, and the development of innate capacities;
- characterized by individualism and competition; which in turn is
- balanced by the conscious cultivation of tolerance and a love that leads to concern for others, and the development of capacities for being of service to society.

Economic Life

The primary purpose of economic life is to meet the earthly and spiritual needs of human beings in a way that respects the spiritual dimension of the human being and nature. Rudolf Steiner recommends gradually replacing the impersonal market, which is based on self-interested behavior and competition, with collaborating associations of producers, distributors, and consumers that will make informed decisions out of mutual interest. Thus, the term associative economics has come to be connected to Steiner's economic ideas although he never used the term himself.[39]

From the perspective of a threefold social organism, the initial motivation in economic life is not self-interest and individualism, as in a healthy cultural life, but rather altruism—caring for others. This becomes manifest through collective or group decision-making processes by those actively involved in economic life. This fact in no way contradicts the importance of entrepreneurial creativity and individual initiative in the economy. Through economic associations, creative entrepreneurs gain awareness of the consequences of their intentions and actions; individualism can thus better serve the wider interests of the community.

Through these trans-sector associations the actual participants in the economic process at hand (or their representatives, depending on the size and scope of the associations) will make decisions, such as determination of quantities to be produced, pricing, allocation of resources, and quality standards. More will be said about trans-sector economic associations in Chapter 8. The directing of the economic process by associations should not be misconstrued as centralized planning in a socialist sense. Rather, economic planning and decisions are made by freely-formed groups of people who are actually involved in economic life, ranging from the local all the way to the international level.

Through such collaboration, we can work toward an economic life that focuses on meeting the real needs of consumers rather than meeting needs instilled in people through corporate advertising aimed at creating new markets.

Whereas cultural life is anchored in the development of thinking, economic activity—producing goods and services for others—is rooted in the soul element of will. Moreover, whereas cultural life cultivates innate capacities brought through the gate of birth, the soul attitudes of fellowship, brotherhood, and servant leadership developed in economic life are the social building blocks for future human evolution. In the economic realm, what we produce—goods and services—has bearing on the future in an earthly materialistic sense, and how we conduct business—the soul attitudes and motivation of those engaged in business—has bearing on the future evolution of humanity in a spiritual, ethical, and moral sense.

Business or economic activity is characterized by doing, making, processing, transporting, communicating, providing services, and so on. In order to prosper, such activities need technical expertise, efficiency, and the intelligent division of labor. While multiple perspectives are required for making the most appropriate economic decisions at a given time and place, provisions also need to be made for private initiative and the entrepreneurial creative spirit to produce goods and services in an innovative and efficient manner, based on these collective insights.

Therefore, we can view a socially responsible economic life as:

- comprised of the associations of producers, distributors, and consumers that support all three spheres—cultural, rights, and economic;
- related to the soul function of willing and to the kind of work that meets material and spiritual needs of human beings;
- based on altruism, caring for others and the environment, and the soul attitude of fellowship, all of which carry on into the future;
- characterized by private initiative and entrepreneurship;
- balanced by cooperation, collaboration, and interdependence.

Rights Life

We now consider the middle realm that weaves between cultural life and economic activity: the realm of human rights, politics, and law. Here the main focus of activity is not personal development (as in cultural life) or working efficiently (as in economic life) but rather on healthy and just human relations. The aim and emphasis in the rights life is the forming of guiding principles for the conduct of our affairs in all types of life situations and activities. These guiding principles involve, for example, fairness, respect, and civility, and they range from personal standards of conduct, or self-government, to legally codified proscriptions, agreements, public health and safety regulations (including environmental protection), and physical security. Ideally, political and legal decisions are determined democratically and should be applied in a consistent fashion to all three realms.

In a healthy threefold society, equality is the prevailing ideal and guide in the rights realm, just as individualism and uniqueness hold sway in cultural life, and collaboration and efficient production are the foundation of economic life. The experience of equality as a member of a democratic society in the realm of rights is essential for human dignity and self-worth, regardless of a person's race, gender, religion, ethnicity, cultural capacities, occupation, position in a community, and so on.

In an appropriately organized, democratically-based political state, we are continually oscillating between self-interested behavior and a concern for others and for the greater community. Wanting a say and asserting one's rights are expressions of self-interest. At the same time, as a democratic citizen, I am obligated to ensure that other people's rights are upheld, and to yield to the decision of the majority once all voices have been heard.

The establishing of rights is related to the soul function of feeling. How people feel about each other and about the various groups within their community is reflected not only in the laws that are created, but also in how the laws are applied and enforced. To the degree that members of a democratic society ennoble their feelings toward their fellow human beings, laws will evolve in a positive direction. Laws and their enforcement can degenerate if antipathies and prejudices override care and understanding. Thus it becomes obvious that while an independent spiritual-cultural realm is not the place to create rights, it is needed to engender the ethics and values that are crucial for the healthy functioning of democracy and government.

The rights realm in a threefold society is:

- comprised of recognizing and upholding human rights through voting, legislation, and law enforcement, as well as non-codified social awareness and qualities such as civility and respect;
- related to human relationships and the soul function of feeling and the need for its continual refinement;
- based on the democratic principle of equality for all;
- balanced by individuals yielding to majority rule and the obligation to uphold the rights of others;
- characterized by dignity, respect, and a sense of each person being an equal and worthy member of a community.

Social Imbalances: Displacement, Intrusion, and Rates of Development

By gaining an understanding of the threefold nature of social life, we can develop the ability to diagnose the root causes of social illness and also to prescribe an effective remedy for either a chronic or an acute situation. We can, for instance, understand the extent to which motives and activities in our society have become displaced from a sphere where they are legitimate and appropriate to another sphere where they are not. Whenever such displacements occur, social illness inevitably arises in some form or other. For example, self-interested behavior and competition, appropriate for cultural life from a threefold perspective, are currently entrenched as the foundation of modern business and economic life. The inevitable consequences of this misplaced egoism and competition are excessive greed and human and environmental exploitation.

The intrusion of the interests of one sphere into another is the root cause of many of our social ills. In particular, economic interests today dominate nearly every aspect of life to the detriment of the whole. Corporate interest groups and lobbyists (economy) virtually control our U.S. Congress (politics); the rulings of the World Trade Organization (economy) take precedence over the laws of nation-states (politics); and big business (economy) dictates federal education reform (politics and culture), to mention a few examples.

It should be apparent why Rudolf Steiner maintains that the social problems of our time are first and foremost issues of spiritual-cultural development. No meaningful change can occur economically or politically if ethics, morals, values, and capacities do not advance to an equal degree. In our age, all three spheres need to advance, but the swift development of an independent spiritual-cultural realm is of primary importance. Humanity is suffering from the fact that the economic life has developed at a far faster rate than the other two spheres of social life. As a consequence, the economy has insufficient ethical and legal guidance from the cultural and political sectors. The economy needs to be guided by and assimilate what the spiritual-cultural and the rights life develop and offer if it is to attain the character of altruism and fellowship. This means, for example, that economic interests should no longer be allowed to use their financial power to obstruct or weaken legitimate environmental regulations and laws or to dictate education reform. As long as this domination occurs, the spiritual-cultural life cannot foster the spiritually creative forces and ideas needed to counter the one-sided, hence destructive tendencies inherent in economic life.

At any given moment people are affected by and participate in all three spheres, regardless of the sphere in which they are primarily engaged. Wherever individuals are active in social life, they are at the same time continuously benefiting from their culturally-derived capacities, are under the restriction and protection of the democratic state, and are supported by the products and services provided by the economy. Thus, the unity of the threefold social organism expresses itself in every individual life.

Chapter 5

The Fundamental Social Law:
A New Foundation for Economic Life

Steiner's economic ideas can in one way or another be related to what he referred to as the Fundamental Social Law. We will now consider this Law not only as a theoretical concept but also as a spiritual tenet that needs to be practically applied in all aspects of business and commerce in order to attain true social responsibility in economic life.

 ❧   ❧

Ants and bees instinctively live by it; indigenous peoples still refer to it; great spiritual leaders have always known it. And modern humanity needs to learn it anew. The Fundamental Social Law asserts that cooperation, mutual aid, and a concern for others benefit society more than self-interested behavior, competition, and the desire for personal gain.[40] This Law is in stunning contrast to the assumption that reigns in market economic theory and practice, that the more people are enabled to operate out of self-interest and competition, and to accumulate personal profit, the more society as a whole will prosper.[41]

Steiner began speaking and writing about this social maxim as early as 1905. He refers to it in various ways throughout his work, calling it "a fundamental principle taken from the spiritual world that underlies social science and social life on a large scale," "an ancient tenet of spiritual science," "the most ancient theme of every esotericist," and "a law that works as surely as the laws of nature."[42]

We can express the Fundamental Social Law in contemporary terms as follows:

The more that individuals work for the benefit of society or the needs of others, and the more that each person is supported by others to lead a dignified existence, the greater the well-being and overall prosperity of a society will be.

As individuals we can try to apply this Law in our daily life and work, but application of this idea on a broad scale will lead to the transformation of virtually all of our social institutions. Such changes would affect our educational system from kindergarten to graduate school, legal forms of corporate ownership, economic markets, financial institutions, and government. Some examples of working in this direction will be given in this section.

Our dominant social institutions aid and abet competitive self-interest and the desire for personal profit. They thwart individual and group efforts to work out of inner ideals and altruism to a degree that prevents the Fundamental Social Law from becoming effective in social life on a large scale.[43] There are many examples of major institutions in all three spheres that thwart the development of altruism in economic life. Publicly-traded stock companies, in which management has the fiduciary obligation to maximize shareholder profits; political parties that are beholden to economic interests; and government education insofar that it promotes self-interest and competition, are examples of major institutions that thwart the development and application of altruism.

Despite these phenomena, an astonishing number of socially, civically, and environmentally responsible initiatives have sprung up over the last few decades worldwide with relatively little public notice. This radical shift in human consciousness and intention is documented in notable works such as *The Great Turning: From Empire to Earth Community* by David Korten and *Blessed Unrest: How the Largest Movement in the World Came into Being and Why No One Saw It Coming* by Paul Hawken.[44]

Although he makes no reference to the Fundamental Social Law, Daniel Pink in his most recent book: *Drive: The Surprising Truth of What Motivates Us*, has uncovered scientific data that supports the idea that people naturally want to work for a cause greater than self-interest and that they are often more productive when they do so. Pink describes three levels of human motivation: biological (thirst, hunger, and so on), responding to rewards and punishments, and intrinsic motivation. Intrinsic motivation has three aspects. "(1) *Autonomy*—the desire to direct our own lives, (2) *Mastery*—the urge to get better and better at something that matters, and (3) *Purpose*—the yearning to do what we do in the service of something larger than ourselves."[45] Furthermore, Pink concludes that human beings "by nature, seek purpose—a cause greater and more enduring than themselves" and that it is important to maximize the possibility for people to work out of a greater purpose in order to "rejuvenate businesses and remake our world."[46]

Rudolf Steiner maintains that the Fundamental Social Law should be viewed not merely as an ethical aphorism but, more importantly, as a law of human interaction and a necessary foundation for building a new economy based on associative cooperation and caring for others. We will consider some corollaries to the Fundamental Social Law referred to in his writings, particularly those concerned with economic life.[47] They are presented here as propositions to be considered in relation to the reader's own experiences in the context of the present financial, environmental, cultural, and democratic crises that humanity faces today.

Poverty, want, and suffering caused by economic arrangements are the result of self-interest or egoism.

The more that people in a given society or community work out of self-interest or personal egoism, the more poverty, want, and suffering will become manifest, even if this connection between them is not readily apparent. Those who are directly involved in a given exchange may not be immediately affected. However, the shirt or the food that I buy so cheaply today may have been produced under conditions of human and environmental exploitation in a distant developing country, and the cost of the environmental damage that occurred in producing it may be passed on to future generations. Today, we can say with some surety that excessive egoism and greed are major contributing factors to environmental and human exploitation and the resultant environmental crisis we are facing.

Social institutions and communities are a reflection of the attitudes, thoughts, and feelings of the people who created and inhabit them.

Socially responsible institutions result only from the thoughts and actions of socially-minded people who exhibit social sensitivity and social skills. Antisocial institutions are the result of antisocial thoughts and feelings. Overcoming the antisocial features of an organization or a community requires more than simply making external changes in governance or administration or improving outer conditions for workers. Equally important is that the people who work in, manage, and even invest in organizations and communities must continually strive to overcome their own antisocial tendencies by purposefully ennobling their thinking and feelings.

Interest in others is the foundation of social life.

Progress toward an economy permeated with social responsibility is dependent on people's cultivation of increased interest in others in all aspects of economic life. Consumers need to develop interest in those producing and delivering their goods and services; producers need to be concerned with the real needs of their consumers; and investors need to be interested in the well-being of workers. The dynamics of a competitive market inhibit individuals from extending ever more interest in other people, whereas such interest can be continually fostered in associations comprised of producers, distributors, and consumers in a given industry, and in regional and international associative networks.

**Developing a greater interest in others requires
the ability to think in pictures.**

We need to picture the effects of economic transactions on people and
nature, and not think about them abstractly. That means as consumers, for
example, being able to picture the situation of those who produce goods and
services on our behalf—their work conditions, and their level of income.
We also need to picture the effects of our purchases on nature, including our
water reserves and animal life. For example, a different picture arises when
purchasing milk from an organic or biodynamic farm as compared to a large-
scale industrial operation.[48] Such imaginative thinking brings us closer to
other people, while abstract economic thinking tends to make us insensitive
and indifferent to the conditions and needs of others.

An associative economic life based on the Fundamental Social Law
requires an educational system and cultural life that foster imaginative or
pictorial thinking rather than focusing exclusively on abstract or indifferent
thinking. It is important to note here that the development of imaginative
thinking is an essential aspect of Waldorf education.

**In order to overcome self-interest or egoism,
a person needs a comprehensive spiritual worldview.**

Neither a fragmented materialistic worldview nor religious dogma can
engender sufficient inner power to overcome egoism and greed in economic
life. Economic necessity, the struggle for existence, and brutal competition
can only be countered with the power generated by a spiritual worldview that
illumines the complete nature of the human being, the origin and evolution
of the universe, the interconnectedness of all beings and activities in the
world, and the role that economic life has and will play in earthly evolution.
A comprehensive spiritual worldview can provide a sense of meaning for each
individual's destiny and can support people in understanding how to make
the best of the circumstances in which they have been placed.

Organizations and communities need a spiritual mission that can be experienced by all participants.

Abstract ideals and theoretical mission and vision statements provide little motivation for an individual to overcome self-interest. All tasks need to relate to a spiritual mission in a concrete way.

Workers and community members need to feel and know the part they are playing in the progress of humanity, whatever their task may be. People can overcome personal ambition and competitive instincts only through freely engaging in a great cause of their own choosing embodied by an initiative or community of which they are a part. As Booker T. Washington, a former slave and founder of the Tuskegee Institute, said in his autobiography:

> In order to be successful in any kind of undertaking, I think the main thing is for one to grow to the point where he completely forgets himself, that is, to lose himself in a great cause. …In this way in the same degree does he get the highest happiness out of his work.[49]

The spirit of an organization or community needs to be felt by all participants. To the degree it is not, egoistic antisocial forces will prevail.

Fruitful cooperation and effective group collaboration depend on the attitude with which people meet and interact.

Every human gathering or association is an opportunity to express and manifest spiritual ideals. However, the more people are divided by prejudices, self-interest, personal ambition, or competition, the less this is possible.

The spirit of a community can become a living reality for its members when they can experience human fellowship. In this sense, economic life can provide countless opportunities for the forming of human associations that can help accelerate the re-spiritualization of the earth and human institutions. Working in harmony with the Fundamental Social Law and the principle of cooperation in economic life will require a new art and science of conversation and human interaction. In turn, this will require attentive listening with the soul and speaking out of spiritual insight, truthfulness, and sensitivity. Over the last few decades there has been an impressive amount of research and development in this direction, including various techniques such as *Appreciative Inquiry, Focused Conversations, Non-Violent Communication, Theory U, World Café,* and *Goethean Conversation.*[50]

Antisocial forces need to be counterbalanced by the continual fostering of social forces within the human being.

Both social and antisocial forces reside in the human soul. However, as ever-increasing individualism becomes part of modern human evolution, the natural consequence is that egoism and the antisocial forces have grown ever stronger. These forces need to be counterbalanced by strengthened social forces. Social forces can be fostered in three ways: (1) through an appropriate education of children that strengthens not only a child's individuality but also social understanding, social sensitivity, and social skills,[51] (2) through adults' taking up specific inner exercises,[52] and (3) through the creation of outer social forms and structures that encourage social responsibility.[53]

If people are to work for society instead of for themselves, they will need to feel that they are equal and worthy members.

People's sense of dignity and self worth, along with the quality of their relationships within their community, depend to a large degree on whether they can feel in some way that they are equal and worthy members, regardless of their position, title, or responsibilities. This fact leads us to the sphere of rights and highlights the significance of democratic equality. The experience of human equality, a feeling that one's essential worth is equal at some level to everyone else's, is a vital prerequisite for enabling a person to work altruistically, out of a concern for others, in a community.

Labor is a rights issue, not an economic issue. All workers have a right to receive a living wage.

Even if individuals live out of a spiritual worldview, and the organization or community of which they are a part has a spiritual mission, they can still be forced into the egoistic struggle for existence if they do not receive sufficient income to meet their basic needs.

In a threefold social organism, the support of workers would not be subject to the forces of supply and demand of the market. Ultimately individuals would work for society rather than simply working for money. The ideal is to not to sell one's labor for the highest possible price, but to remove human labor from the commodity market altogether.

All workers who labor on behalf of society to meet expressed needs, regardless of position or title, have a right to a decent income, an income sufficient to meet the basic necessities of life and to lead a dignified existence in keeping with the general standard of living of a given society. In a healthy society, this would be a fundamental democratic right that all economic enterprises take as a given just as they take as a given the availability of natural resources. However, this right should not be construed as a guaranteed wage for capable people who are unwilling to work even though they consume goods and services produced by others.

In order to ensure human dignity for all concerned, to encourage cooperation, and to foster motivation consistent with the Fundamental Social Law, workers and management alike would be treated as co-producers and share in the overall proceeds of production. In so doing, they will both need to share appropriate responsibility for the efficiency of production and the quality of goods and services produced. Productivity and efficiency in the future will need to become ethical responsibilities freely carried by all workers and management for the common good.

Vocation and socially responsible ideals need to unite.

The desire to do something meaningful in life is a significant inner experience that wells up when a person develops a sincere interest in current events and the plight of fellow human beings and the environment. In the future it will become increasingly important for people to feel harmony between their inner and social ideals and their outer work. This harmony will be undermined if, through social circumstances or economic necessity, a person is compelled to work solely (and soullessly) for money. Henry David Thoreau spoke eloquently on the issue of meaningful work and appropriate income in the following way in the essay, "Life Without Principle":

> The ways by which you get money almost without exception lead downward. To have done anything by which you earned money merely is to have been truly idle or worse. …
>
> The aim of the laborer should be, not to get his living, to get "a good job," but to perform well a certain work; and even in a pecuniary sense, it would be economy for a town to pay its laborers so well that they would not feel that they were working for low ends, as for livelihood merely, but for scientific, or even moral ends. Do not hire a man who does your work for money, but him who does it for love of it.[54]

Human labor has evolved over time from tribute and slavery to serfdom, and currently to paid labor for many people. Looking to the future, Rudolf Steiner foretells that to the degree that people are able to unite their vocation with inner ideals on the one hand, and receive an adequate income on the other, work will become freely given and develop into a sacred service done on behalf of humanity in response to genuine needs.

The love of work and a concern for humanity and social life are essential learning goals in an educational system working in harmony with the Fundamental Social Law.

From a cultural perspective, it is a legitimate form of self-interest or egoism to want to fully develop one's individual capacities. Furthermore, the people who can best serve humanity are those who do develop their capacities to the maximum. Therefore, enabling students to actualize their full potential, giving scope and direction to all their individual gifts and talents, is an essential task of education. At the same time, the development of a love of work and of sensibility for the needs of others also must be a focus of a modern educational curriculum. It is a healthy social instinct, even a moral responsibility, to feel an obligation to give back to society at least in proportion to what we have received. Those who are more capable should give more, and those who are less capable will give less.

Training, whether in farming, business, education, art, religion, research, or other vocations, needs to illumine why and how a particular work serves humanity, to encourage character development, and to develop an understanding of the Fundamental Social Law and the threefold nature of social life.

In general, the fostering of social forces in the human soul will require an educational system independent of economic and political influence, one that supports the development of spiritual, ethical, moral, and artistic capacities in addition to academic skills.

Working for others is inherent in the division of labor.

The division of labor that necessarily prevails in a modern economy means that it is not possible to simply work for oneself in an outer sense. The results of the work we do are not our own but are given over to the total production process. Through the division of labor we become part of a united effort to create a complete product or service. Inherent in the application of the division of labor in any economic activity is a kind of outer altruism. Even so, workers act against this altruism insofar as they are working for personal gain out of economic necessity or personal ambition.

The organizing principle for an economy working in harmony with the Fundamental Social Law will be neither impersonal competitive markets nor a centralized state, but a new third way of organizing economic activity: associations of producers, distributors, and consumers collaborating together.

Associations of individuals and groups—the actual stakeholders in the various sectors of production, distribution, and consumption—who share perspectives and information will organize economic activity. Such associations, formed in freedom, will foster conscious collaboration and fellowship rather than instinctual self-interest and competition. Individuals and networks of associations will determine the allocation of resources, the quantity, quality, and types of goods and services to be produced, and the appropriate prices. We can see the beginnings of such associations and activities in the community supported agriculture and fair trade movements. We will consider these and other examples in more detail in Chapter 8.

Appropriate or "true prices" arise when workers receive sufficient income to meet their needs and those of their dependents.

Workers should receive sufficient income to meet their own and their dependents' needs while they are producing a product or providing a service for society. The price to be charged for the product or service—the true price—will arise through negotiations among producer, distributor, and consumer associations. Factors that affect prices in relation to these sectors are the needs and wants of consumers, the right of workers to an appropriate minimum income, and worker efficiency. These negotiations, in turn, rest on the healthy relations of the three sectors of society: cultural, political, and economic. Chapter 14 will consider true price more extensively.

In reality, it is not money but the work of others that sustains us.

Hidden behind every transaction or exchange is an untold amount of human labor. Failing to recognize that it is the labor of other human beings—not money—that allows us to live indicates a lack of interest in the well-being of others. With every gift, purchase, or loan we participate in we express our interest or lack of interest in our fellow human beings.

Since we live by the labor of others, we can recompense society only through our own labor. In the future, people will need to develop the social sense to recompense society, to the degree they are able, with products or services of an equivalent value to what they have used. The fact that monetary wealth can increase in the possession of capable individuals who have not contributed an equivalent value to society is an indication of social illness and injustice. Such individuals gain undeserved economic power to command labor for their own needs or selfish desires. We can recognize here the antisocial nature of wealth gained through speculation in real estate, stock, and currencies.

Money should diminish over time and be reissued.

If money is to be a medium of exchange and the basis of an accounting system that accurately represents the circulating values of commodities and services, its life cycle or durability should coincide with the nature of the commodities and services that it represents. Commodities wear out and services are used up over time, unless they have been worked on, refurbished or extended in some way through human labor and ingenuity. If it is to remain true to its nature and purpose, money itself should also wear out or diminish in value over time and be issued anew. This should occur not through a general inflation of prices but through measures such as dated currency and periodic reissues.[55] The overall amount of money needs to increase or decrease according to the goods and services in circulation or soon to be in circulation.

Some observed effects of time-dated currency are an increase in the circulation rate or velocity of money and a reduction or elimination of hoarding. Christian Gelleri, manager of the popular time-dated regional currency Chiemgauer in Germany, has demonstrated that the Chiemgauer circulates at three times the rate of the Euro.[56]

Land and other means of production should be treated as community assets, not as commodities to be bought and sold for personal gain.

Real economic values and resulting wealth are created through work that meets human needs. Value creation has two aspects: the actual physical labor involved and how skillfully the labor is directed. Steiner refers to these two forms of value creation as "labor transforms nature" and "spirit [intelligence] directs labor."[57] From this perspective, land that has not been improved or worked upon in some way has no economic or commodity value.

Personal wealth gained from buying and selling land is paid for by society as a whole through mortgages and rents. This burden falls most heavily on low-income individuals and businesses who can't afford to purchase land and benefit from rising land prices.

The right to exclusive use of land needs to be considered from both a legal and a cultural perspective. It is a rights issue insofar as everyone requires—and therefore has a right to—access to land, if only to have a home. In addition, capable people who want to use land to produce something of benefit to society ought to have the exclusive right to use it for however long their activities are deemed beneficial. To gain exclusive ownership of land through personal economic power and then to sell it for personal profit turns land rights into land abuses. The escalation of land prices owing to land speculation is a significant contributing factor to the spread of poverty and the uneven distribution of wealth.

The determination of how land is to be used and who is to have use of it should be made through the collective wisdom of the local community, which is a cultural capacity based on knowledge and experience.

What is true for land is equally true for human-made means of production such as work facilities and machinery: Neither should be treated as a commodity or personal property, but rather they should be considered as community assets rather than personal assets. Whereas undeveloped land is "God given," a human-made means of production arises through complex factors and relationships in the economic process involving the whole of society. This does not mean that land and other means of production should be owned or controlled by the government. Rather, they should be held in trust for a community by a non-profit corporate entity. Community land trusts are an example of a legal vehicle that can remove land, structures, and capital equipment from commodity circulation and make them available to capable people for productive use through lease-type arrangements.[58] Another legal structure that secures property and means of production on behalf of a local community are community-owned department stores.[59]

Chapter 6

The Transformation of the Competitive Market and Capitalism: Building an Associative Economy

We will now review the main features of the modern market economy and contrast them, feature by feature, with an associative economy that is consistent with a threefold social organism and the Fundamental Social Law. As described above, at the heart of this new economic approach are collaborating associations of producers, distributors, and consumers (or their representatives) that would determine the types, quantity, and quality of goods and services to be produced and their appropriate prices. Questions concerning scarcity of resources would be addressed by human experience and intelligence rather than by impersonal market forces.

One should give full recognition to the fact that capitalism and the competitive market have together played a significant role in the advance of modern civilization. In economics alone this includes the great advances in the division of labor, technology, entrepreneurial innovation, and the accumulation and transfer of capital. We must give equal recognition, however, to the fact that modern capitalism has contributed to human exploitation and environmental destruction to an extent that is no longer acceptable. Meeting the environmental and social challenges of the 21st century requires that we find a way to address these issues fully. The question is how to do so in a manner that retains the beneficial aspects of modern economic life.[60]

The Transformation of the Competitive Market and Capitalism to an Associative Economy

FROM	TO
Materialism	Spiritual Holism
The Economy as Dominant Sector	An Economy as One of Three Vitally Important Sectors
Self-Interest and Egoism	Altruism
Profit Motive	Social Needs Motive
Instinctual Competition	Intentional Collaboration
Invisible Hand Ethics	Ethical Individualism and Social Responsibility
Impersonal	Personal
Divisive	Inclusive and Participatory
Unregulated Supply and Demand	Associations Overseeing Supply According to Demand
Investor Needs as Primary	Consumer Needs as Primary
Labor as a Commodity	Workers as Partners and Co-Producers
Means of Production as a Commodity	Means of Production as a Community Resource
Wealth without Production	Wealth through Production
Inequitable Distribution of Wealth	Fair Distribution of Wealth
Money as a Commodity	Money as Bookkeeping
Prosperity through Accelerated Growth	Prosperity through Creative Thinking, Ingenuity, and Financial Acumen
Emphasis on International Trade	Emphasis on Diverse Multi-level Trade

Illustration 2

Associative Economics: Spiritual Activity for the Common Good by Gary Lamb
© 2010 AWSNA Publications

From Materialism to Spiritual Holism

The development of the modern market coincided with the rise of materialistic thinking, especially since the late 1700s. From a certain perspective the modern economy can be viewed as applied materialism.[61] Economic thinking that is influenced by materialism and based on self-interested behavior tends to be shortsighted and to focus on immediate gratification, with little or no concern for distant peoples, places, or future generations. Because of the apparent need for constant economic growth, mainstream economics places a large emphasis on the material and purported psychological needs and instinctual desires of investors, producers, workers, and consumers.

A new associative economy based on social and environmental responsibility requires spiritual, ethical, and moral considerations to be brought to bear on all facets of economic life. It would be based on the development of higher-order faculties of thinking, feeling, and willing that go beyond mere instinctual competition and egoism. A deep conviction regarding the inherent interrelatedness of all people and nature in a transcendent whole will help increase tolerance for differing viewpoints and will encourage personal responsibility for one's actions in all spheres of life, including business. This does not mean imposing any type of religious dogma on people. Rather, it implies the upgrading of all actions by means of enhanced individual ethical capacities and personal conduct.

From the Economy as the Dominant Sector to an Economy as One of Three Vitally Important Sectors

In today's age of materialism—with its focus on earthly possessions, individual comforts, and personal gratification—it is inevitable that economic life has become viewed as the most important aspect of life. This view pervades not only our economic life but our judicial and legal system and cultural life as well. The dominance of economic considerations corrupts democracy and freedom. Competing players in the economy use their resources to influence elections and legislation to give them an advantage in the market. Thus, elected officials who accept special interest funding become beholden to those interests rather than to the citizenry.

In contrast, in a healthy threefold social organism, the economy is one of three equal and vitally important aspects of society. It does not dominate the democratic political system, which provides the guidelines for human relations, or the spiritual-cultural life, which is the source of our ethics, morals, and creativity and gives direction to our overall development. All three spheres of activity are necessary and fulfill important functions for the full development of each individual and humanity as a whole. More specifically, in order for economic life to fulfill its task of providing goods and services without exploiting people or the environment, it needs the guidelines of an independent democratic realm and the ethical insights and creativity arising from an independent cultural life.

From Self-Interest and Egoism to Altruism

Bill Gates, who has enjoyed the dual privilege of being the wealthiest person and the most powerful philanthropist in the world, spoke about two "great forces of human nature: self-interest and caring for others" at a recent meeting of the World Economic Forum.[62] We do not argue with this view of the human being. However, it is time to challenge the most significant defining feature of the modern market economy—that is, the belief that self-interested behavior must be the foundation of any prosperous modern economy. This belief is instilled worldwide, even in economically underdeveloped countries, through the media and most school curricula from the lower grades through graduate school.[63]

Gates, like so many others, refers to Adam Smith's *Wealth of Nations,* published in 1776, to validate this perspective.[64] Even so, he candidly admits that the competitive market is not serving much of the world's poor and urges businesses to become proactive in meeting their needs. Even as he does so, however, he advises that they should not change by "one iota" their belief in the benefits of self-interested behavior as the driving force for economic life.[65]

As described in the two previous chapters, the associative approach to economics is based on the Fundamental Social Law: that is, overall prosperity and long-term economic sustainability can best be achieved by acting out of a concern for others and cooperation. Conversely, human and environmental exploitation are the result of personal egoism and self-interested behavior.

From Profit Motive to Social Needs Motive

If self-interest is the engine that drives the modern economy, then the desire for profit is the fuel. The late Nobel Laureate economist Milton Friedman maintained that in a free market economy "there is one and only one social responsibility of business—to use its resources and engage in activities designed to increase its profits so long as it stays with the rules of the game."[66]

In direct contrast, in an associative economy, any surplus capital beyond covering appropriate costs of production can at best be viewed as one indicator of successfully meeting a real need, but never as the primary motivation for engaging in business in the first place. The entrepreneurial spirit will still be valued and encouraged, but that spirit will focus on social needs rather than personal profit. Workers and management will be viewed as partners and co-creators of goods and services, and therefore the proceeds of enterprises will be divided accordingly.

From Instinctual Competition to Intentional Collaboration

Competition is a chief characteristic of the modern market, at least in theory. Its proponents generally assume that an unregulated competitive market is the most efficient and socially responsible means for determining prices, allocating resources, and providing the maximum number of choices for consumers. History has certainly proven the superiority of the competitive market over a socialistic command economy. However, it can be readily observed that as an industrial or service sector matures, capital concentrates within fewer and fewer businesses and competition diminishes. Consider, as examples, the banking, oil, finance, automobile, and even the natural foods industries.

A significant by-product of this concentration of capital in the hands of self-interested, competitive people and businesses is the proliferation of corporate-financed political interest groups. These interest groups undermine our democratic institutions. (See Chapter 17 for more on interest groups.) Thus, capital is the basis not only of economic power, but corruptive political power as well. Furthermore, in the cultural realm, competitive instincts have been elevated to a status of virtue and are widely fostered in our educational institutions through such things as high-stakes testing and sports.

As explained in the previous chapter, in a healthy social organism, competition as we generally understand it would find its rightful place in the cultural realm. However, within this context, free competition would be transmuted and elevated from an instinctual drive to informed decision-making for the benefit of society.

From the Invisible Hand Ethics to
Ethical Individualism and Social Responsibility

The theory of mainstream market economy holds that public good is the unintended result of competition and self-interested individualism. Adam Smith maintains as much in *The Wealth of Nations*: that is, public benefit results not so much from the intentions of publicly-minded people as from the striving for personal profit. The accumulated productivity of the self-interest of many individuals is transformed into societal benefits and public good by an "invisible hand." Thus Smith and his adherents ascribe a certain morality that is beyond human nature and human intention to the market itself. Smith asserts that human beings don't have the requisite intelligence to direct economic life.[67]

In contrast, from the perspective of social threefolding and associative economics, it is precisely through ethical individuals working collaboratively for the good of others in economic associations that human beings can give direction to the economy and the greatest good can be achieved.

Ethical individualism, meaning the development of self-directed individuals who are ethically responsible, needs to be cultivated in a cultural life that is independent of the dictates of profit-driven business interests. An education system free of such interests can focus on fostering a wide range of human traits and capacities beyond self-interest and instinctual competition.

From Impersonal to Personal

So-called competitive markets are understood to be impersonal. Economist Milton Friedman describes it this way:

> There is no personal rivalry in the competitive market place. …The wheat farmer in a free market does not feel himself in personal rivalry with, or threatened by, his neighbor, who is, in fact, his competitor. The essence of a competitive market is its impersonal character. [68]

Friedman's point is that the market is an arena of impersonal competition rather than a personal rivalry between two or more individuals, and this is salutary. According to Friedman, market competitors can have only a negligible influence on prices through "the combined effects of their separate actions."[69] This thinking is abstract and disconnected from reality. We must recognize that the modern competitive market is not merely impersonal; it fosters ignorance and cold indifference about the effects of one's economic transactions. In contrast, an associative economy is highly personal, given that producers, distributors, and consumers are encouraged to know and understand each other's situation through their associations. We have already noted that they will necessarily confront the social and environmental effects of their own intention and activities, whether they are buying or selling, lending or borrowing, donating or receiving.

From Divisive to Inclusive and Participatory

The features of today's market tend to separate people, organizations, and sub-sectors within the economy. Rather than openness and transparency, these features promote deception and secrecy within organizations and through covert business and government alliances. This is for good reason: What your competitors know about you can give them an advantage in the market. Consumers compound this separateness by being socially uninformed and mainly concerned with price rather than people or environmental conditions on the other side of an exchange.

In contrast, associations of producers, distributors, and consumers are inclusive and participatory by design. They encourage sharing of information and collaboration among all active participants so that a complete economic picture can arise concerning the products and services under consideration. This includes consumer needs and purchasing capabilities on the one side, and the capacities and needs of the distributors and producers on the other.

As already mentioned, in an associative economy workers and management work as partners in the creation and distribution of goods and services.

From Unregulated Supply and Demand to
Associations Overseeing Supply According to Demand

A conventional free market is considered to be a highly efficient self-adjusting mechanism that achieves optimal prices by providing an arena for the forces of supply and demand to freely interact with one another. According to its advocates, interventions such as subsidies and tariffs interfere with its inherent capacity for achieving efficient pricing and allocation of resources.

An associative economy would rely on neither state regulations nor an unregulated competitive market to achieve appropriate pricing of goods and services. Rather, prices and the amount and type of goods and services to be produced would be determined by participants with real-time knowledge and experience in the economic process: producers, distributors, and consumers who freely associate with each other. The economy would be embraced and directed by human mindfulness and collective actions.

By and large, associative economics supports the ideal of free trade, but not to the detriment of people or the environment. A business sector working with the ideals of a threefold social organism would take as a mandate what the democratic sector determines as just and environmental protection regulations.

From Investor Needs as Primary to Consumer Needs as Primary

Although publicly traded stock companies comprise only a small percentage of businesses, they account for a majority of all business activity. In addition, the primary fiduciary duty of their management is to maximize shareholder wealth. As a consequence, the market economy is primarily an investor-driven economy. In contrast, it is interesting to note that even Adam Smith in *The Wealth of Nations* maintains that the primary purpose of economic activity is to meet consumer needs, not the needs of producers.[70]

The starting point for economic associations in a threefold society will be the legitimate needs of the consumers who are informed about the real impacts of their purchases on the people who provide them. The main purpose of business will be to meet those needs in an efficient manner.

From Labor Treated as Commodity to
Workers as Partners and Co-Producers of Goods and Services

From a typical accounting perspective, human labor is viewed as a cost of production, something to be purchased like any other commodity. Admittedly, this is an improvement over the slavery, indentured servitude, and serfdom of former times, when the human being itself was treated as a commodity. We must now make a further step in the evolution of labor:

In an associative economy, an essential guiding principle is that workers are treated as partners with management. Those who labor in any and all aspects of production should share accordingly in the proceeds of the business.

This new perspective removes labor from the commodity circuit and places it under the full protection of the rights sphere insofar as minimum income and benefits, work conditions, and duration of work are concerned. Thus, in a threefold social organism the goal is to enable workers to work freely on behalf of society rather than selling their labor in order to make a living. The motivation or incentive to work will arise from qualities such as those described in the chapter on the Fundamental Social Law: a sense of social responsibility, a love of work, and a feeling that one is contributing to the betterment of the world.

From Means of Production as Commodity to Means of Production as Community Resource

In the modern market economy, land and other means of production are considered private property and treated as commodities that can be bought and sold for personal profit. Indeed, speculation on land and on real estate has proven a very effective means of creating and accumulating wealth in modern society. As stated in the previous chapter, from a threefold perspective land has no commodity value unless it is worked on in some way. Consequently, the land itself should not be considered a commodity, but rather a community resource and asset overseen by some type of trust or not-for-profit organization based in the cultural realm rather than the economic domain.[71]

Likewise, human-made means of production—buildings and machinery, for example—would be treated as community resources that have been built up by untold numbers of people within the economic life of a community or region. These means of production need to be made available to entrepreneurs who will produce goods or services for society. Thus, the means of production would be community assets, not private property, that is privately managed for the benefit of society. The transfer of the means of production would not occur through a purchase based on financial resources or by inheritance (unless the heirs are deemed capable of continuing the operations), but by decisions of the trustees acting on behalf of the community with input from the outgoing entrepreneurs of the means of production.

As mentioned in the previous chapter, the community land trust model is one legal form that can facilitate such arrangements.[72] Typically there is a board of trustees comprised of lessees, local community members, and people with professional expertise such as lawyers, accountants, business people, and builders.

From Wealth without Production to Wealth through Production

Today's modern market economy creates a substantial amount of wealth that is not connected to the production of goods or services. This includes speculation in land, stock, and currency. Thus, some people can accumulate vast amounts of wealth without contributing an equivalent amount of value back to society. This wealth then acts as capital debt that needs to be settled through a general inflation of prices and rents and new investors who pay ever higher prices until the system collapses. Real estate speculation is a prime example. For decades it was safe to assume that real estate values would continually rise, regardless of whether any property improvements were made. Thus, it was possible for savvy, and even not-so-savvy, real estate buyers to simply buy a property and resell it after a short period of time at a sizable profit. This general increase in property values devoid of property improvements—phantom wealth—has an inflationary effect on rents that affects most strongly low-income families and small businesses that do not own their own homes and business sites. With the recent decline in real estate prices in today's economic recession, there are a growing number of homeowners who are defaulting on their mortgages.

Most speculative wealth creation is in reality a Ponzi scheme in which money from new speculators is used to pay off earlier speculators.

In an associative economy, economic values and the accumulation of wealth would primarily arise through the production of goods and services needed by society. Phantom wealth created through speculation and the creation of valueless services would be eliminated.[73]

From Inequitable Distribution of Wealth to Fair Distribution of Wealth

In his previously mentioned speech at the World Economic Forum, Bill Gates candidly acknowledges that the market serves only those who can pay, and that philanthropy and government agencies try to help those who cannot. He also maintains that philanthropists and government don't have enough resources to address all the needs of the poor. Gates then appeals to the business leaders of the world to try to find profitable ways to address the needs of the poor without giving up the principle of self-interest. He calls this refinement of the market activity "creative capitalism."[74]

Rather than trying to encourage business leaders to creatively activate their self-interest to address the inequitable distribution of wealth that they themselves have helped to produce, an associative economy would provide for a more equitable distribution of wealth to begin with.

Methods for ensuring a fair distribution of wealth have already been mentioned: (1) the state, unencumbered by special interests, would establish appropriate living income laws for workers and provide for the care of the aged and the infirm (see Chapter 11); (2) the means of production would be treated as community resources rather than private property that can be sold for personal profit; (3) workers and management would be treated as partners and co-producers of goods and services, and the proceeds would be shared accordingly; and (4) entrepreneurs who put their abilities in service to the community and increase community assets would be rewarded to a limited degree by those benefiting from such assets. Ultimately, the possibility for capable people to accumulate wealth without providing society with an equivalent amount of values in return would be eliminated.

From Money as a Commodity to Money as Bookkeeping

In today's market economy, money is more than a medium of exchange; it is also treated as a commodity with fluctuating values and as an object of investment. Rudolf Steiner argues that the appropriate functions of money are as a medium of exchange and as a measure of value that can serve as the world's bookkeeping system. As a medium of exchange, the money supply should be related to the total value of goods and services in circulation and the anticipated additional goods and services to be produced in the foreseeable future. As a measure of value, specific units of money should be related to economic values, meaning the amount of labor it takes to produce specific goods. He suggests the amount of labor to produce a certain amount of wheat as an example of an appropriate unit of measurement for a currency.[75]

Steiner also maintains that the quality of money changes as it circulates. He describes different qualities for three differing uses of money: purchase money, loan money, and gift money. One function of economic associations would be to monitor the flow of money and stimulate the economy by helping to direct purchase, loan, and gift money to where they are needed at the appropriate times and in the appropriate amounts. For example, they could connect consumers with capable producers, lenders with entrepreneurs in need of credit, and donors with cultural organizations in need of financial support. He also suggests that rather than increasing in value through interest income and speculation, money should wear out like the goods and services that it represents. Thus, money should be time-dated and reissued as needed according to the overall state of the economy and future production requirements.

From Prosperity through Accelerated Growth to
Prosperity through Creative Thinking, Ingenuity, and Financial Acumen

It is generally understood that the modern market is dependent on accelerated growth to maintain prosperity. Consequently, the rate of economic growth must continually increase or economic decline will quickly ensue. The necessity for accelerated growth is variously ascribed to compound interest rates or wealth generated through speculation instead of production. Regardless of the reasons, growth mantras prevail—such as "the economy must grow," "growth is the key to solving poverty," "grow in order to stay competitive"—and businesses feverishly expand and pursue new markets.

From the perspective of associative economics, growth is healthy as long as it is a result of increased production meeting real needs. Increased demand should draw increased production. However, manipulating consumers to buy more goods and services, with consequent exploitation of workers and the environment, is counterproductive to the goal of prosperity. Active associations can determine what the real needs of consumers are and use that information to adjust expansion of production accordingly.

We need to find sources of renewal for economic life other than accelerated growth and mergers. Rudolf Steiner maintains that the primary source of rejuvenating economic life is an independent spiritual-cultural life that is outside the control of economic interests. Without spiritual renewal, economic life becomes destructive to the other spheres of human activity. A rightly organized threefold social organism will enable each generation to develop its innovative capacities and ideas for social renewal rather than educating it to conform to outdated thinking.[76] An independent cultural life would be a continual and unlimited source of creativity, inspired thinking, and moral capacities that radiate into the economic and political spheres. These capacities can never be fully realized within a cultural life and an educational system that are controlled by corporate interests and their political counterparts. Rather, true economic and social renewal are dependent on all individuals having the opportunity to unfold their potential, including a full range of intellectual, social, and practical skills that in turn can be applied to economic life. People's creative, ethical capacities will find fulfillment in economic associations comprised of participants in economic life who are well-informed and motivated by a genuine interest in others.

There is another important means of economic renewal that can emerge in an associative economy. As explained, these associations will facilitate ongoing conversations between producers, distributors, and consumers and will have access to up-to-date data and knowledge of the financial needs of each economic sector involved. Thus, they will be in a position to help businesses and financial institutions continually to stimulate the economy by ensuring that the right amount of purchase, loan, and gift money will flow in a timely manner to where it is needed the most.

From an Emphasis on International Trade to an Emphasis on Diverse Multi-level Trade

Following World War II, representatives of leading nations met in the United States at Bretton Woods, New Hampshire, to facilitate ways for countries to strengthen their economies. They focused on fostering international trade and reducing trade barriers. The result was the formation of such organizations as the World Bank, the International Monetary Fund, and later the World Trade Organization. The emphasis on international over domestic trade has dominated economic thinking ever since. Consequently, developing countries have been encouraged, if not required through loan agreements, to focus almost exclusively on exporting to the world market. While such a focus helps certain sectors of society, providing world markets with new raw materials and consumers with cheap goods, these outcomes have often come at the expense of local agriculture, businesses, and indigenous cultures.

Just as a viable natural ecosystem thrives when all levels of life from the simplest to the most complex interpenetrate and interact with each other, so too, in order for a healthy economic organism to meet the needs of all constituents, a diversity of trade and markets will be required. Rather than focusing exclusively on international trade and exports, an associative economy would naturally develop local, regional, national, and international trade.

Chapter 7

Trans-Sector Economic Associations: Earthly and Spiritual Potentials

In democratic societies, the science of association is the mother of science; the progress of all the rest depends on the progress it has made.[77]

– Alexis de Tocqueville, *Democracy in America*

The great art form of America is government and especially the Constitution. … and in this art form, it seems to me, America is pointing to the most essential art form of the future, the art of working together as individuals, groups and communities. This is the essential art form of coming humanity—the art of human association.[78]

– Jacob Needleman, *The American Soul*

Both individualism and associations of people voluntarily working together on a common cause or task have deep roots in American culture. The Frenchman Alexis de Tocqueville wrote about this phenomenon in *Democracy in America*, published in two parts in 1835 and 1840. He recognized that strong individualism, so important for a democratic society, needs to be balanced by more social characteristics. This can be accomplished through working together in associations, which he called "the mother of science."

Feelings and opinions are recruited, the heart is enlarged, and the human mind is developed, only by reciprocal influence by men upon each other. I have shown that these influences are almost null in democratic countries; they must therefore be artificially created, and this can only be accomplished by associations. [79]

Tocqueville identified voluntary associations in all sectors of nineteenth century American life, for example: businesses in economic life; parties, interest groups, and opposition groups in political life; and religious, moral, entertainment, and educational associations in cultural life. Like Tocqueville, Jacob Needleman, who has a modern perspective, asserts the prime importance of associations for the future of America, even though he calls it an art rather than a science.

One of Steiner's most significant contributions to economics has been to extend and deepen the concept and the applicability of the principle of association. He did this on two levels: earthly and spiritual. In regard to the earthly, he showed the importance of extending the scope of voluntary associations in the economy from single businesses, professional trade organizations, or consumer associations to embrace all three aspects of economic life: production, distribution, and consumption. Earlier types of economic associations tended to rely on self-interest or self-promotion—generating profits, promoting a trade or industry, or buying more cheaply. The chief purpose and distinguishing feature of trans-sector economic associations is that they aim to develop cooperation among all three economic sectors and arrive at fully informed and mutually determined decisions that can be implemented in an efficient manner. These associations, consisting of actual participants (or their representatives), would collectively and mutually determine such things as prices and amounts, types, and quality of goods and services. Thus, economic decision-making would be conducted by people with direct knowledge and experience of the matters at hand. Unlike the price-fixing that sometimes occurs in the modern market, whereby various producers collude secretly to keep prices artificially high in order to gain greater profits at the expense of consumers, the determining of prices within trans-sector associations involves participants in a transparent open process of fully informed agreements. Some may object that although worthy, this is a highly impractical goal. However, in terms of the technical aspect, working associatively or collaboratively is no more complex than conducting operations in the modern market. The production, communication, and distribution challenges are similar to a large degree. The key difference is not technical but social: The motivation of participants in associations is concern for others rather than self-interest, and information is shared with openness and inclusiveness rather than secrecy and divisiveness. Trans-sector economic associations already exist, if only in elementary stages, on both the local and international levels.

Community Supported Agriculture (CSA) projects, which number in the thousands in the United States, are an example of associative multi- or trans-sector collaboration on a local level.[80] They are based on mutually agreed upon commitments between farmers and a local community of consumers. The types and quantities of products and finances are determined on an annual basis through ongoing dialogue between both parties. Live Power Community Farm in Covelo, California, for example, describes its CSA approach as an "association of involved consumers and dedicated farmers. The farmers provide a weekly basket of fresh, high-quality vegetables in season while the shareholders commit their financial and volunteer support for a minimum of one growing season."[81]

CSA farms have increased in number and size, and the CSA movement has developed many associative practices and innovations that extend beyond a single farm. For instance, rather than a single farm attempting to produce all the products for its community, production has been shared among one or more farms through formal or informal contractual arrangements. Also, we have seen the development of a distinct distribution function as shared production has emerged and when farms establish off-farm distribution sites for consumer groups or home delivery routes.

While it is clear that the CSA movement is successful in creating ongoing dialogue between farmers and consumers, some people doubt that such a collaborative and highly personal way of working is possible on a regional let alone an international scale. Admittedly, size is an important factor to take into consideration when developing economic associations. However, economic associations can also be effective on a larger scale through representatives working on behalf of each sector and through the networking of various associations. In any case, the viability and dynamics of an economic association is definitely influenced by its size. If it is too small it will not be economically viable, and if too large the exchanging of perspectives and communication between the various sectors may be hampered and become overly time consuming. But these are natural and healthy parameters. The actual workings of the association will determine the manageable limits for a given industrial or service sector. In contrast, the conditions we now face in the current economic arrangements are the result of the fact that there is no inherent market mechanism to determine appropriate size limits on the upper end. Rather, the whole economic system has become dependent on businesses that are supposedly too big to fail and as a consequence require massive government bailouts if they appear to be faltering financially.

The CSA movement has focused mainly on local food production, which in the northern part of the United States may be only be a small percentage of a family's total food consumption in a given year. An important question is: Could the CSA associative model be the basis for a much more extensive domestic or even international economic food supply chain that can supply a significantly greater portion of a family's food needs?[82] The answer is yes. It will become increasingly possible to develop associative relations on a much broader basis as the CSA movement grows in any given region of the United States. Let's say that within a 75-mile radius there are 10 CSA farms with an average of 100 participating families.[83] Let's also assume a conservative figure of 2 persons per family. That yields a consumer base of 2,000 people. These CSA families could associate together and assess their collective non-CSA food needs. Based on these statistics they could form a regional consumer association and contract with local food processors and farms further south, where the growing season is longer, in order to meet a larger portion of their food requirements. Such a consumer group could also associate with specific farmers or cooperatives in Central and South America to produce coffee and tropical fruit rather than relying on the impersonal market. These same consumer families would be in a position to set up and invest in their own low-interest capitalization fund that supports the farms and distributors within their associative network. In this scenario we can see how an extension of the CSA movement could help transform the food economy from competing businesses to collaborating associations of farmers, distributors, and consumers.[84]

There are in fact numerous examples of businesses, distributors, and consumer groups working associatively on an international level, if only in an elementary way. The Fair Trade movement is developing distribution systems with fair prices while assisting farmers and craftspeople in developing countries to market their products to consumers in more industrialized nations. Equal Exchange, a worker cooperative in Massachusetts and pioneer of fair trade coffee in the United States, is one example of this.[85] Equal Exchange acts as a distributor and processor for small farmer cooperatives that use sustainable farming methods in developing countries. They currently offer coffee, tea, chocolate, and snacks with annual sales of over $20 million. Part of Equal Exchange's social mission is to establish prices that are fair to farmers and to foster closer connections between consumers and the farmers they rely on. In keeping with this mission, as a distributor Equal Exchange enters into dialogue with the farm cooperatives to learn about their needs, to determine a fair price for their products, and to assist them in achieving quality production standards suitable for international markets. Equal Exchange is also active in educating consumers in the United States about the farmers who produce the products they consume by arranging for farmers from other countries to meet with consumer groups in the U.S. and by creating informative point-of-purchase materials.

Another example of businesses working associatively on an international scale is the organic cotton supply chain set up by the Swiss-based trading company, Remei AG.[86] Under the leadership of Patrick Hohmann, Remei AG has developed a supply chain of associated businesses based on cooperation and transparency, beginning with several thousand small organic cotton farmers in India and Tanzania. Remei AG markets organic cotton thread, yarn, and clothing worldwide, including clothing for the Naturaline eco-label of Coop Swiss, a Swiss consumer cooperative network with over two million member consumers.

Steiner's description of the expansion of the principle of economic associations to include all three sectors of production, distribution, and consumption has its counterpart on the spiritual level. In this regard he points to the significance of working together in associations for the spiritual advancement of humanity as a whole. Alexis de Tocqueville also referred to the benefits of participating in associations for the individual—the expansion of heart and mind—and for the group—mutual understanding by all participants.

Steiner goes further by taking into consideration the attitude or disposition of soul that a person carries into the dialogues and activities of associations. The spoken word in conversation is the artistic and scientific medium for modern associations. From a spiritual perspective, every human association—whether it be a congregation, school, political party, business, or informal gathering—is an opportunity to collaborate with higher powers. The collective feelings of the participants in the group stream together to create a vessel for divine beings to connect with the activity. The intentionality, level of attentiveness, and the quality of feelings and thoughts that a group of people bring to a gathering will determine what kind and degree of spiritual support they will attract while working together. The phrases national, community, and team spirit take on real meaning when considered from this perspective. Even more so does the statement by Christ, "When two or more are gathered in my name, there am I in their midst." [87]

Steiner describes the spiritual dynamics of associations in the following way:

> When human beings find themselves together in voluntary associations, they group themselves around centers. The feelings streaming in this way to a center … give beings the opportunity of working as a kind of group soul. …Indeed, in a certain respect we may say that they support their existence on human harmony; it will lie in individual souls whether or not they give as many as possible of such higher souls the opportunity of descending to humanity. The more people are divided, the fewer lofty souls will descend into the human sphere. The more associations are formed where feelings of fellowship are developed in complete freedom, the more lofty beings will descend and the more rapidly the earthly planet will be spiritualized.[88]

While voluntary associations can be formed in any realm of life, it is economic life that provides untold opportunities for creating local associations that can be networked globally. Economic life can thus provide a unique opportunity for the planet to be spiritualized by caring people worldwide freely associating together to meet the needs of human beings.

From everything said above regarding Steiner's ideas on trans-section economic associations, we can conclude that they:

1. Re-establish the principles of unity and inclusiveness in economic life.

The introduction of the division of labor has enabled a tremendous increase in human productivity and has created the conditions for machinery and technology to arise. However, the division of labor and the factory system have brought divisiveness at many levels. The worker has become alienated from his work, management has become a distinct activity separate from labor, and owners and workers have become separate classes of people with differing perspectives on life and work. Economic associations bring about a unifying effect in economic life, whereby producers, distributors, and consumers collaborate together and share perspectives in mutual respect.

Through their associative workings they achieve understanding for the whole economic process. Furthermore, workers and management are viewed as co-producers or partners in production of goods and services.

2. Infuse work with meaning and purpose.

Prior to the division of labor, a worker had a direct relation to his products and often to the people for whom they were intended. Specialization and the factory environment have made it difficult to derive meaning and satisfaction from work itself or the partial product produced. Through economic associations, workers can perceive the value and importance of their work for the community of people they are serving. Thus, work becomes meaningful through social awareness.

3. Introduce human intention in economic life.

Proponents of the market economy view it as a self-regulating system that operates best with no human or state intervention through such measures as tariffs, subsidies, and price regulation. Economic associations allow the producers, distributors, and consumers who are involved in the economic process to match production with expressed needs of consumers. This can involve adjusting the supply of goods and services, establishing quality standards, and determining the best distribution system. Thus, the market is not left to its own devices as in a so-called free market, nor is it directed by people who are not involved with the economic process under consideration, as in socialism, but through fully informed participants.

4. Instill social awareness and responsibility in economic decisions and activities.

When various participants of economic associations come together to work through economic decisions a social awareness arises that is not possible in the market economy. Participants not only have the opportunity to express their perspectives, wishes, and needs but also are confronted with the views and needs of others in the context of the whole economic process. This awareness is supported by ethical capacities developed in the independent cultural life.

5. Promote openness and transparency.

Trans-sector economic associations as described here are designed to make economic decision-making and activities open and transparent, not only to the actual participants but to the broader public as well.

Chapter 8

Freedom, Funding, and Accountability in Education

One of the least appreciated tenets of a threefold social organism is the necessity for the emancipation of education from government control. Nonetheless, we must understand today why separating school and state is just as important a cultural goal for a free and democratic society as the separation of church and state was previously.

Even most advocates of systemic social change never question the idea that government education, commonly known as public education in the United States, is the pillar of democratic society. In discussions on educational freedom the assumption is made that such freedom can be somehow created within the vast structure and oversight of the state.

Corporate interests are actively and openly sought by government education reformers to help shape government education reform. For the last three decades education reform, which includes the implementation of national goals, standards, and assessments, has been the collaborative effort of the federal government and big business. The Goals 2000 Educate America Act and the No Child Left Behind Act, created by Democratic and Republican administrations respectively, are nothing more than financial and corporate interests and thinking codified into law.[89] Consequently, virtually all education reform has become subjugated to the apparent necessity of accelerated economic growth at the expense of all other cultural and democratic needs.

Numerous interest groups, most significantly teachers unions, actively oppose any attempt to develop an education funding system that might result in reducing the role of the traditional local public school in educating children. Their opposition is understandable. Recent studies have shown that the educational landscape in the United States would change dramatically if all parents could choose the school they think is best for their children instead of most of them being compelled by financial constraints to send their children to the local public school. Currently, from 85 to 88 percent of children are educated in government schools. According to recent surveys conducted as part of independent research in six states sponsored by the Foundation for Educational Choice [90] (see Illustration 3), parents, if enabled to do so, would choose the following schooling options for their children:

Private School:	39%
Charter School:	11%
Home School:	10%
Local Public School:	38%
Virtual School:	1%
Don't know:	>1%

Taking these results as an indication of what parents really want for their children, private schools and home schools would account for approximately 49 percent of elementary and secondary education school children, instead of the current 13.5 percent; and government schooling—local public schools and charter schools—would account for approximately 49 percent, instead of the current 86.5 percent. This clearly presents a path to improving education, including increasing parental involvement in education, student graduation rates, and teacher innovation. That path begins and ends with parental choice in education.

From a social threefolding perspective, we can acknowledge that government education as the means of educating children had a useful purpose for a period of time. However, the time has passed for it to be the

Current US Student Distribution vs. Parent Preferences

Comparison of current student population according to type of schooling vs. parent responses in 6 states to the following question: *"If it were your decision and you could select any type of school, what type of school would you select in order to obtain the best education for your child?"* (Numbers indicate percentage of affirmative responses).

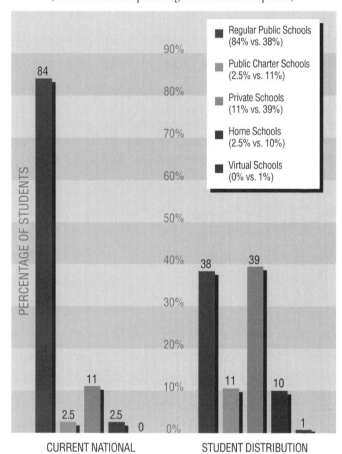

*Sources: Private and public schools: Council for American Private Education; Charter schools: National Alliance for Charter Schools; Home schools: National Ctr. for Educational Statistics.

**Based on 3614 surveys conducted in 2010 in Alabama, Arkansas, Kansas, Mississippi, New Jersey and New York. Surveys sponsored by The Foundation for Educational Choice and conducted by Braun Research, Inc..

Illustration 3

main means of educating children, as the parent responses to the surveys confirm. To persist in compelling the majority of school-age children to attend specific schools contrary to the better judgment of their parents has become one the greatest injustices suffered by the American public. It is also one of the greatest threats to political democracy and cultural freedom in modern times.

It is essential that activists in the field of alternative economics begin to understand the importance of educational freedom and the necessity for developing new forms of funding education that allow all parents to choose the education they think the most appropriate for their children. Not to do so is to say to all parents: The state knows what is better for your children than you do.

The following aphoristic statements provide a basis for freedom, funding, and accountability in education from the perspective of a threefold social organism, a basis that would provide independent schools an equal opportunity to offer their services to the public.[91]

Inclusive public education should be more than just government schools.

A well-educated public is essential for a democratic society. Educating the public or public education should not be restricted to a specific type of school or schooling system. Government schools, independent schools, religious schools, and home schooling all need to be viewed as valid approaches to educating the public. An intermediate step toward separation of school and state is to reduce the role of government schooling from a public requirement for most families to a public option available to all families, an option that is eventually funded in the same manner as all other schools.

Every child in a democratic society has a right to a decent education.

The right to a decent education needs to be recognized and upheld as an equal opportunity for all children. Compelling families to send their children to schools that are unsafe or clearly unable to meet their educational needs is a denial and abrogation of such a right. Regarding education, a society's primary legal obligation is to its children and their rights, not to a particular school or a schooling system. Society's obligation to uphold the right of all children to a decent education means first and foremost that all parents of school-age children should have the financial resources to provide them with a decent education; otherwise that right is meaningless. For most families this right has devolved to compulsory attendance at a local public school whose educational goals, standards, and assessments are determined by the state.

**There needs to be one financially level playing field
for all types of schooling.**

All families should have financial resources sufficient to ensure their freedom to choose from a variety of local schooling options for their children, whether government, independent, religious, or home schools. The financial viability of a school should depend ultimately on its ability to win the confidence and appreciation of parents and students rather than on the government's determination of which schools or types of schools should receive funding and the use of power to compel families to send their children to them. In other words, parents, as their children's representatives, should have the ultimate say concerning which schools should exist, not legislative bodies or political interest groups.

**The independent school movement would welcome the opportunity
to educate children from all economic backgrounds.**

Independent schools have been unfairly limited in their ability to educate children from low- and middle-income families because of outdated state funding mechanisms. In general, Waldorf and other types of independent schools would welcome the opportunity to have greater diversity in their schools and to serve a much broader public.

An equitable and efficient funding system for education is an essential component of a free and democratic society.

An equitable funding system would not place a disproportionate burden on those who have the least ability to pay. The ideal funding system is one that collects and distributes funds efficiently in a transparent manner and does not burden schools with undue regulations. Funding programs based on education tax credits are examples of an efficient and cost-effective means to enable families of all economic backgrounds to select the type of education for their children that they think is most appropriate. Various states have enacted education tax credit legislation, including Arizona, Florida, Georgia, Indiana, Iowa, Pennsylvania, and Rhode Island.[92] The Public Education Tax Credit model legislation developed at the Cato Institute allows individuals and businesses to contribute directly to schools or scholarship programs on behalf of a child's tuition and receive a tax credit applicable to a variety of taxes. The fact that these types of tax credit programs do not involve government funds, but rather encourage private sector funding instead of public (tax) money to uphold a child's right to an education removes a major justification for the attachment of onerous government regulations to education tax credit legislation.[93]

Teachers should have the freedom to teach out of personal knowledge and classroom experience.

The world is changing. Social conditions are changing. Human consciousness is evolving. Consequently, education needs to be an evolving art and science. Each child is unique, and each new generation has new capacities, interests, and challenges. Teachers need the opportunity and freedom to be innovative and respond based on their direct insight to the needs of each child and to the changing conditions of the world. In turn, each upcoming generation needs the opportunity to develop the insight and capacities to improve and, if necessary, transform the existing economic and political systems, not simply fit into them.

Independent schools should have the freedom to set their own educational goals, standards, and assessments.

Independence and freedom in education is meaningless if all schools are compelled to adhere to the same values, goals, standards, and assessments dictated by a centralized authority. Independent schools and home schoolers, in particular, should have the freedom to establish their own goals, standards, and assessments, and create their own accrediting associations. Otherwise their status as independent has no significance. Eventually, all schools should have this freedom.

Independent schools should be accountable to the families they serve, the accrediting bodies they choose, and the state where they are located.

Independent schools that fully inform their school families about their educational goals, curriculum standards, and assessment methods would be judged by their performance. In a free and just society, they would have the freedom to create and be held accountable to independent school accrediting organizations that they choose. It is appropriate that independent schools abide by appropriate state laws and regulations regarding safety, upholding of contractual commitments, the unacceptability of hate-based factions and fraud, and fair employment practices.

Real competition in education is the key to providing the best education possible for all students.

In summation, real competition in education is the most efficient way to give parents of all financial and cultural backgrounds the opportunity to become actively involved in their children's education. This will enable the most valued educational approaches and schools to succeed, and ultimately will allow all children to have the best education possible.

Chapter 9

The Economic Necessity for Educational and Cultural Freedom

A Human Perspective

Along with fostering the all-important qualities of precision, efficiency, and timeliness, the modern market economy is also dependent on certain "lower" human attributes prevailing in business and commerce. These attributes include self-interested behavior, competitive instincts, a craving for personal power, and an insatiable desire for material goods and comfort.

In contrast, an associative economy as a part of a threefold social organism as described here would rely on and even foster a greater array of higher-order capacities and virtues than what the modern market requires. These traits include an interest in and care for other people and society as a whole, a love of work, and an appreciation and respect for nature.

An essential step in ensuring the development of higher-order attributes is to liberate cultural life, including education, from political and corporate influence. As an apparent educational tool, state-mandated norm-referenced high-stakes tests tend to limit education, and hence general human development and culture, to a narrow set of human qualities primarily focused on what is needed to sustain the existing market economy.[94]

We should not educate our children with the goal of fitting them as economic beings into the competitive economy, as if this were the most important aspect of life. Human beings are spiritual as well. Nor should we make the presumption that government and big business know more about educating children than educators in the classroom, or accept that they know what type of schooling is better for a given child than the child's parents. Enabling the human spirit to come to full development out of its own nature and resources—a necessity of our time—requires that education establish its own independent administrative bodies and develop its own goals, standards, and assessments rather than having them dictated by state agencies that are in turn heavily influenced by big business.

An Economic Perspective

Economic life itself needs to be viewed as a living organism that is subject to the same laws as all living organisms. One such law is the need for continual rejuvenation in order to maintain life. Historically, the market has relied on accelerated growth and mergers to revitalize what was assumed to be an open-ended economy, as the business maxim "grow, merge, or die" implies.[95] In a desperate attempt to assure continued growth and forestall economic decline, businesses engage in the following types of activities:

- Enter into ever-larger mergers;
- Lobby to remove environmental protection laws to reduce immediate manufacturing costs and maintain cheap access to natural resources;
- Continually move factories to countries where labor is less expensive;
- Expand markets by turning everything possible into a commodity, including public water supplies and plant species;
- Increase consumer demand by using the media to intensify the desire to own and consume new and ever-larger amounts of goods and services;
- Increase future market efficiency by inculcating self-interest and the desire for profit in children through educational goals and standards collaboratively developed by big business and government;
- Downsize the number of workers and force those who are left behind to increase their workloads.

We are now in a one-world global economy, and a new source of rejuvenation must be found for economic life. From a social threefolding perspective, human beings educated in an independent spiritual-cultural life that encourages development of their full personal and social capacities are themselves the ultimate source of these rejuvenating forces. One capacity that is essential for continual renewal of the economy is creativity. Ken Robinson, a world-renowned expert in human creativity, makes the case that government-sponsored education reform programs, including the U.S. No Child Left Behind program, which was largely designed by big business, actually kill creativity and minimize the importance of such creativity-building activities as the arts in education.[96]

Steiner maintains that each rising generation brings with it essential regenerative forces that the economy needs; otherwise it will self-destruct.

> The economic thinking of the present is a destructive element, which must, therefore, be continually counterbalanced by the constructive element of the spiritual limb [cultural realm] of the social organism.
>
> In every generation, through the children we teach at school, something is given to us, something is sent down from the spiritual world. We take hold of this in education—this is something spiritual —and incorporate it in economic life and ward off its destruction. For economic life, if it runs its own course, destroys itself.[97]

An economic system that dictates a society's education policy and culture through the coercive powers of the state is on a suicidal track. It will cultivate only those capacities and skills needed to perpetuate the existing economic and political order, and in doing so economic life will strangle the source of its own creative life forces—the inexhaustible fount of human capacities and creativity arising from cultural life.

Chapter 10

Individual and Cultural Freedom

The educational development of an independent, self-directed human being who can bring rejuvenating forces to economic life through entrepreneurial initiative and creativity, social sensitivity and skills, and ethical certitude is contingent on four educational and social factors. All four must be taken into consideration in any effort to develop an authentic and independent cultural life and educational system consistent with a threefold social organism.

Liberty

By liberty we commonly mean political independence or freedom from outer restrictions and control by the state. However, the ultimate source of political oppression can be cultural when, for instance, fundamentalist religious groups impose their dogma on society through laws of the state. Or oppression can be rooted in economic life through the lobbying of corporate interest groups. Indeed, the greatest modern-day threat to liberty is in fact rooted in the economic sector, notwithstanding the fact that a healthy economic life itself requires entrepreneurial freedom and initiative. For example, modern political life and government education are a reflection of economic interests and economic thinking to a degree that is detrimental to democracy and culture. It is commonly recognized that politicians, regardless of party affiliation, are little more than marionettes whose strings are manipulated by corporate interests and financiers. This is made possible through the fact that wealth and its attendant power are concentrated in a relatively small number of people and groups. Because of the unholy alliance that exists between financial interest groups and government, such economic wealth has come to represent not only economic power but cultural and political power as well. These pockets of concentrated economic power in the social organism are similar to a human organism besieged with tumors. Initiatives working in harmony with the principles of a threefold social organism are hygienic measures that combat such unhealthy concentrations of wealth and help ensure the maintenance of cultural freedom.

Full Development of Capacities

We have recognized that the primary function of cultural life is to enable the development of human capacities to the fullest possible extent. Individuals cannot become self-directed human beings and exercise freedom of will as long as their innate capacities remain dormant. Although the intent of national- and state-mandated norm-referenced, high-stakes tests is to improve student performance and to measure progress toward educational goals, such testing serves little or no educational purpose other than grading and ranking students according to a very narrow set of learning goals.[98] To the degree that this is true, such tests actually have a crippling effect on future economic productivity insofar as potential capacities that are not measurable by such tests are left undeveloped. As a noteworthy exception to this crippling trend, Waldorf schools, which decline to administer standardized tests, place significant emphasis on developing creative imagination and social skills—both of which are essential capacities in an associative based economy.

Overcoming Inner Obstacles

Even when individuals are blessed with liberty, their exercise of free will can be undermined owing to personal soul weaknesses or obstacles such as uncontrolled passions, fearfulness, inability to concentrate, insensitivity, or the lack of self-worth. These may be inherited or externally inflicted traits.

One of the main goals of any true education toward freedom is to help students overcome these types of soul weaknesses. If such weaknesses or tendencies are not or cannot be addressed pedagogically, then they may develop into more severe problems that will need to be addressed medically later on.

Economic Dependency

The full development of an individual's potential can also be compromised by insufficient financial resources. This can occur in two ways. The first is the obstruction of access to educational opportunities through inadequate financial resources. Under the current system in the United States, parents with insufficient income are often forced to send their children to schools they do not think are adequately educating their children. The second obstruction is the hindering of the application of developed capacities. This occurs, for example, when capable entrepreneurs who want to produce something of value for society cannot obtain the necessary capital or means of production to do so. For instance, it is often impossible for young farmers to obtain loans to expand their enterprises because they do not have sufficient collateral according to conventional banking practices. In both these cases the impeding of individual aspirations or contributions results in thwarting the rejuvenation of economic life. The education of all children to their full potential and access to capital for individuals who want to meet a recognized community or societal need are key features of the threefold social organism and priorities in an associative economy.

Chapter II

Rights and Single-Payer Systems for Education and Health Care

Steiner's ideas on the funding of education are another departure from the thinking prevalent today among sociologists, economists, politicians, and indeed the general public. The commonly held view is that education is the responsibility of the state, and therefore the state should determine what is most worth learning and doing in life, and that government should fund education through tax revenues. Steiner maintains, however, that education should be funded directly by economic life (see Illustration 4) rather than by means of a single-payer (that is, the government) system financed by tax revenues (see Illustration 5). Traditionally in the United States, these funds have been given primarily to local public schools, which have been the only option for the vast majority of families who could not afford other options such as independent schools, parochial schools, or home schooling.

Steiner's indications for education funding follow from his recognition and affirmation of the right of every child to an education, meaning that every child should have an equal opportunity to a decent education rather than being compelled to attend a particular government school. He also takes the view, which is not an unusual one, that tax revenue, which is public funding, requires public oversight even in a democratic society. Consequently, it is appropriate for the state to regulate education if it provides for its funding. All state-funded projects are of necessity subject to majority rule and attendant bureaucratic regulations. The idea that an independent education system could realistically exist within a state schooling system is contrary to the very nature of both government and independent education. An education system will be independent only if is has an independent administration and operates outside of any political influence. However, the state does have three financial obligations important for upholding the right of every child to an education.

The state needs to determine:

1. the amount of education subsidy that is required from the economy for the education of children on an annual basis;
2. how much each of the various types of businesses and individuals should be obliged to contribute to education;
3. who is eligible to receive such funds, for example, children of a certain age and families within certain income parameters.

In order to arrive at informed decisions on these matters, the state will need to enter into deliberations with representatives of the education and economic sectors.[99]

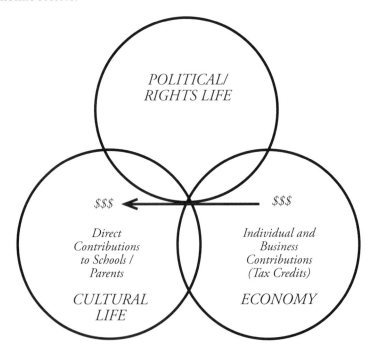

Illustration 4–Funding of Education Directly from the Economy

The education tax credit movement in the United States is one of the more promising steps toward creating an educational funding system that does not rely solely on government funds while still enabling the state to fulfill the three functions just noted. Currently, 11 states have personal tax credits or donation tax credit programs in which individuals or corporations can make contributions directly to scholarship programs or to schools on behalf of children's education expenses.[100] As already mentioned, one of the most innovative recent model education tax credit programs is the "Public Education Tax Credit Act" proposal developed by Adam B. Schaeffer at the Cato Institute.[101] It provides support for a child's education expenses through contributions that are eligible for credits on a variety of taxes, including personal and business income, sales, and property taxes.[102]

Much of what has been said about the funding of education can also apply to funding of health care. Access to basic health coverage should also

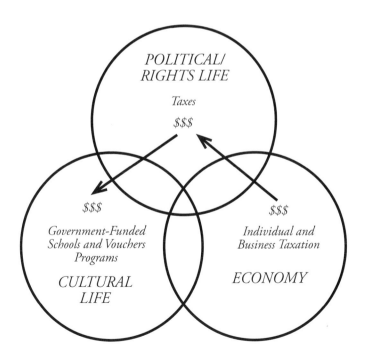

Illustration 5–Government Funding of Education

be viewed as a human right for all people. As in the case of the right to an education, the government has three basic duties in upholding the right to health care: determining the amount of funds the economy needs to generate for basic health care coverage, determining how much individuals and organizations are obligated to contribute to the financing of health care coverage, and who is eligible and how much each person might be eligible to receive for health care coverage.

One possible way to implement this approach is for the economy to contribute a certain amount of money directly into non-governmental health care funds that eligible people could access to pay for health care coverage. As with education, the government's role should be limited to the three functions mentioned, and it need not be the collector or administrator of the funds. Sufficient non-burdensome regulations for both education and health care could guarantee transparency and protection against fraudulent use of funds.

Currently, the right to universal health care coverage is usually equated with a compulsory government-administered and funded single-payer system. This is considered to be the only viable alternative to a voluntary free market approach in which vast numbers of people have no money to pay for health care. What is presented here suggests a third way to uphold the right to health care coverage while allowing for maximum individual freedom of choice both in selecting the type of coverage and medical modality. It must be acknowledged that as long as big business and unions play such a powerful role in our legislative processes, as they currently do now at the state and federal levels, they will use any attempt to change the funding of education or health care as an opportunity to expand their power and influence and create new markets.

Chapter 12

Economic Indices and Basic Human Needs

Our technological age has enabled empirical researchers to generate an enormous range and amount of economic statistics. Some broad categories of economic indicators are productivity, income, prices, employment, wages, credit, and balance of trade. Each category in turn provides an array of statistics. These can be used to validate virtually any political or economic agenda, as demonstrated by the statements of politicians when campaigning for election.

If we decide to work toward a more associative economy, we need to focus at least initially on certain specific economic indicators. If we take as a premise that the primary purpose of economic life is to meet the material needs of human beings, then we can first focus on those key economic indicators that show how well the economy is succeeding in this regard. We should investigate, in other words, to what degree the economy in a given nation or region is meeting the basic needs of everyone within that area by providing affordable products and services.

The following basic human needs of every person should be affordable:

- clean food and potable water,
- housing,
- clean air and sunshine,
- clothing for personal and work life,
- health care,
- education,
- transportation options,
- access to basic communications technology.

The determination of what constitutes the norms for basic human needs in a given area is not the task of the economic sector; rather it is the primary responsibility of the state or rights sphere to determine what the basic needs are for individuals. Obviously, in a healthy society, representatives of the rights sector will need to take into consideration the productivity of the economy when determining what realistically can be provided overall in each category of need. Clearly, the economy is not expected to produce clean air and sunshine, but continuous access to them must be ensured by the state though environmental laws and regulations.

There are two other important economic indicators to monitor. One is the amount of available capital for entrepreneurs who want to provide a product or service to meet an essential need. The current system of finance is structured to capitalize almost exclusively the most economically profitable business initiatives. This system falls short at capitalizing endeavors that meet vital community needs but may yield little profit for investors. For example, a relatively inexpensive natural remedy with ingredients that are readily accessible and easily processed without costly equipment may not find a source for necessary start-up capital, while a more expensive and perhaps less effective remedy that has the potential to yield large profits will attract large amounts of venture capital. The first product may provide a greater benefit for the community through a general improvement of health at a lower cost than the second product that provides less public health benefit but a larger financial return for a few investors.

Thus, it would be a significant economic and social benefit to identify, monitor, and publicize innovative methods of commercial funding that place at least an equal emphasis on social benefit as on amount of return. The Slow Money or Patient Capital movement led by the social entrepreneur Woody Tasch, which focuses on financing agriculture-related ventures, is an example of how to encourage investors to think beyond maximizing economic returns.[103] Some examples of organizations involved in providing capital for community-minded businesses that produce important goods or services which may not necessarily be highly profitable are RSF Social Finance, TBL Capital, and Shore Bank.[104]

Another important economic indicator to monitor is philanthropic giving for cultural endeavors in a given region. This should include not only the amount of money being given to various types of organizations but also who is giving and how much. The problem of significant concentration of wealth in economic life has a social parallel in philanthropy, where certain individuals or foundations control vast amounts of philanthropic assets. Large foundations have an undue influence in determining which cultural initiatives succeed and which do not. Thus they can have a disproportionately strong influence on cultural life itself. Bill Gates, whose foundation has assets of approximately $30 billion, has a huge impact on the role of computer technology in education reform, beyond what any single person or organization should have. No single source of money—individual, corporate, or state—should have such an enormous degree of influence and power over education or any other aspect of cultural life.

In summary, economic indicators in these three areas—individual basic needs, availability of capital, and philanthropy—provide the minimum essential information that would be needed to monitor any effort to transform and continually renew economic life consistent with the principles of associative economics.

Chapter 13

Money and Morality:
From Citizens to Supra-Rulers

The love of money is the root of all evil.
— First Letter from St. Paul to Timothy 6:10

Government and banking have colluded to create a political money system that embodies a "debt imperative" that results in a "growth imperative," which forces environmental destruction and rends the social fabric while increasing the concentration of power and wealth. It creates economic and political instabilities that manifest in recurrent cycles of depression and inflation, domestic and international conflict, and social dislocation.[105]
— Thomas H. Greco, Jr., *The End of Money and the Future of Civilization*

It is important to note that people often misquote the first statement above, saying that money is the root of all evil. Rather it is the love of money that is the culprit. Saint Paul is referring to our relation to money, our love of the power that it represents and what we imagine we can do with that power. Implicit in this thought is that the lover of money is thinking in selfish terms, with little regard for other people or the planet we live on. If it is true that self-centered acquisition and use of money can cause harm and suffering in the world, then it must also be true that it is possible to use money out of higher motives to engage in acts of moral goodness. Again this suggests that money itself is not the culprit, but rather the person who uses it. Indeed, history is replete with abundant examples of individuals doing both good and ill with their money. In our times we have experienced people such as Bernie Madoff, the Wall Street investor and former chairman of the NASDAQ stock exchange, who defrauded individuals and organizations of an estimated $12–20 billion. His greed and lavish life style had no limits. At the time of his arrest in 2008, Madoff's personal assets were valued at close to $1 billion, which included $17 million in cash, a $7 million yacht, four residences worth a total of $22 million, and $12 million worth of jewelry, art, and furniture. For his crimes Madoff was sentenced to an equally impressive 150 years imprisonment.[106]

While this may seem to be an individual case of unusually extreme deception and exploitation, we are now faced with a national, if not world-wide financial crisis that is rooted in the systemic financial abuse of sub-prime mortgages, credit cards, and the unregulated derivatives market.[107] Even so, at the same time that we have this widespread cavalierism and immense greed, we can also identify examples of people and institutions working creatively with money for the good of society, including those mentioned in previous chapters.[108]

However, there is a growing body of research and commentary that suggests that the mechanism of money creation and finance determines to a large degree what individual ethical and social impulses can or cannot flow into social life. We have quoted Alan Greenspan, the former Chairman of the Federal Reserve Bank, as saying that business people have many more ways to express greed in economic life than ever before. Our modern economy is known for concentrating wealth in the hands of a relatively small group of people who are often operators in the financial markets, including banking. To maintain continued domination of our money supply, the privileged, wealthy and powerful few require large sums of capital, the ability to make decisions in secrecy, the ability to manipulate elected officials, and the ability to control education and the media. The proposals presented in this book are an antidote to these kinds of situations. The measures with the most significant impact, however, would likely be those that would minimize excessive and inappropriate concentrations of wealth. Such measures would include:

- decommodifying land and other means of production and treating them as community assets, which can be made available to entrepreneurs working on behalf of society;

- decommodifying money or currency and transforming money into a publicly transparent accounting system;

- in general, eliminating, or reducing to a minimum, wealth creation that does not result from creating products and services with real economic values; this would include eliminating speculation in stock, currencies, and land and the charging of interest or fees for financial services that do not provide anything of real value to society.

One of the goals of an associative economy is to make sufficient capital available to capable entrepreneurs who want to provide something of recognized value to a community. Thus people's capacities and social responsibility will draw capital into circulation, not economic power or personal connections. Surplus capital beyond what is needed to support workers and management and for reinvestment purposes would be considered community assets or used to support cultural life rather than be treated as a private possession to be invested for personal gain or used to gain special privileges. This measure alone would remove much of the power base of any potential supra-ruler.

There is some debate even among critics of our current monetary system as to who should issue currency and how that should be done. The author Ellen Brown recommends that government issue its own currency rather than the banking system headed by the Federal Reserve, and spend it into circulation through such projects as public works. But the unfortunate reality is that neither the banking sector nor the state can be trusted to create money if cultural, economic, and political arrangements remain the same as they are now. Author E.C. Riegel describes the situation like this:

The money mechanism ... is a contrivance that is both political and private but is strictly neither. It is a hybrid, and its name is *finance*. Compounded from both political and private interests, it compromises both private enterpriser and public service. It confounds students of money and causes them to take sides for either the banking end or the government end when in fact a plague should be put upon both their houses. Control over money should be denied to both government and banks.[109]

Greco suggests the establishment of voluntary direct mutual credit-clearing systems as a replacement for the current monetary system that is monopolized by a government-bank oligarchy.

Transforming our existing economic structures can help prevent a relatively few wealthy people from gaining further control of our economy and financial system. However, new ways of using money for antisocial purposes will continue to surface if such outer restructuring such as Greco recommends is not accompanied by the moral elevation of those who work in those structures. When considering the relationship between human morality and money, Rudolf Steiner indicates that a certain level of social awareness and moral obligation eventually needs to arise in all individuals. First of all we need to become aware of the fact that it is the labor of our fellow human beings, not money, which provides us with the necessities and luxuries that we may enjoy in life. And consequently, we need to develop the feeling of obligation to give back to society, while we are capable of doing so, the equivalent value of what we take from the economic circuit. The crux of the relationship is: How we view and use money is a gauge of our interest and concern for others. Rudolf Steiner expresses this thought as follows:

How many people there are today who have an abstract and confused conception of their personal lives. If they ask themselves, for example, "What do I live on?" ... they would say to themselves, "Why, on my money." ... Money is not something on which we can live. ... My money has no value other than that of giving me the power to make use of the labor of others. Under the social conditions of the present time, we do not begin to have an interest in our fellow men until … we hold the picture in our minds of a certain number of persons working for a certain number of hours in order that I may live within the social structure. …No one loves people if he supposes that he is living on his money and does not in the least conceive how people work for him in order to produce even the minimum necessary for his life. …But the thought that a certain number of persons labor in order that we may possess the minimum necessities of life is inseparable from another. This is the thought that we must recompense society, not with money but with work in exchange for the work that has been done for us. We feel interest in our fellow men only when we are led to feel obligated to recompense in some form of labor the amount of labor that has been performed for us. …The feeling of obligation to the society in which we live is the beginning of the interest that is required for a sound social order. …Enjoyment should really never be accepted without repaying its equivalent to the whole of society.[110]

While such thoughts point to the moral capacities that need to be developed in relation to money, they still beg the question of who should issue money. The government? private banks? or free associations of people, as Greco recommends? The direction that Steiner suggests is to remove the issuing of currency from the state and place it within the economy. Money, after all, is meant to facilitate economic production and exchanges. The issuing of money would therefore be closely connected to the operations of economic associations in a threefold society, with their focus on efficient economic processes. Only the implementation of the basic principles of a threefold organism can guarantee financial integrity and efficiency in this regard. In an associative economy within a threefold organism, self-serving interest groups, whether the state or private banks, would not control the issuing of money. Instead, economic associations would enable money to flow efficiently where and when it is needed, keeping money true to its nature as a representative of the economic values in circulation.

Chapter 14

True Price

Every working person should receive sufficient remuneration for a commodity he produces to meet all his and his dependents' needs until he has again produced another such commodity.[111]
— Rudolf Steiner, *Towards Social Renewal*, 1917

A "true price" is forthcoming when a person receives, as counter-value for the product he has made, sufficient [income] to enable him to satisfy the whole of his needs, including of course the needs of his dependents, until he will again have completed a like product.[112]
— Rudolf Steiner, *World Economy*, 1922

In his ground-breaking lectures in *World Economy*, Rudolf Steiner emphasizes the central importance of price formation in economics. When he first uses the actual term *true price* he admits that his formula for a true price "is only an abstraction to begin with."[113] However, he maintains that his main objective here and in other lectures and writings on economics is to relate the whole of his spiritually-based economic science to this initially abstract-seeming concept. For, as we will now demonstrate, all fundamental concepts of associative economics and social threefolding are inherent in what he develops and reveals as the principle of true price.

Three Spheres Cooperating as Equals

Steiner provides two formulations of true price, with commentary, that taken together comprise the foundation of a new economic science that honors the human spirit.

His first discussions of the principle of a true price in 1917 assume certain prevailing conditions that are in harmony with the ideals of a threefold social organism: "Only within a social organism managed on the basis of free cooperation between its three spheres will it be possible to achieve a healthy relationship between price and commodity."[114] It is pointless to try to introduce the concept of true price on a large scale into an economic arena that dominates political and cultural life and, in turn, is dominated by private ownership of the means of production, self-interested behavior, and the desire to maximize personal profit. Under these conditions the needs of a worker will be seen only as an expense to be reduced to a minimum.

For example, present conditions allow the rights of a people to be overruled by economic interest groups with respect to the environment. Prices are artificially depressed or falsified in a given region whenever businesses exploit the environment and pass the cost of addressing pollution and restoring nature's balance on to other nations or to future generations. Even so, steps can be taken toward true pricing to the degree that basic human rights are upheld and whenever a more associative way of working develops within an economic arena. Some examples are fair-trade standards, community supported farms, and ethical investing. Single enterprises can begin working with a triple bottom-line that accounts for people, planet, and profit—rather than profit alone. In so doing, social and environmental factors can begin to be reflected in prices. A step in this direction was taken through the B-Corp certification system for like-minded businesses. A certified B-Corp must meet certain standards of social and environmental performance.[115]

Decommodification of Labor; Workers Treated as Co-Producers

We have noted that one of the features of a new associative economy will be that workers will be treated as co-producers and partners with management and will share the proceeds of the operations accordingly. In both formulations of true price the worker is characterized as an independent entrepreneur or contractor, not a paid worker. Indeed, Rudolf Steiner maintains that we can never obtain true prices if workers are treated or act as mere wage-earners, selling their labor like a commodity.

> Those who to this day are still mere wage-earners—earners of a living for themselves—how are they to be placed in the whole economic process, no longer as such earners but as men who work because of social needs? Must this be done? Assuredly it must. For if this is not done, we shall never obtain true prices but always false ones.[116]

We can conclude from this position that if workers are seen only as a cost to production rather than as co-producers, then the tendency will be to depress their income to the lowest possible amount. This tendency would continually falsify prices in the sense of true pricing.

An essential feature of true price formulation is that it points to the future, not to what has been done or produced in the past. This feature is important for two reasons. One is financial. Looking to the future will give us a more realistic—true to the facts—picture of a person's need for financial support. If we base the anticipated support of workers on past statistics alone, they may receive less than what is needed to produce similar products in the future, owing to changing economic conditions.

The other reason is spiritual. Typically, people are paid an income on a weekly, biweekly, or monthly basis, at the end of a pay period for work already performed. In contrast, true price formulation is based on what a person needs for support in the future. Thus, in keeping with the principles of true price and the Fundamental Social Law, workers should be paid at the beginning of a pay period for work to be done. They would be receiving credit based on future productivity, just as enterprises typically do when they obtain credit for future production. Such an approach to remuneration thus enables or frees people to work on behalf of others rather than selling their labor.

Decommodification of Land and Other Means of Production

Prices can be falsified in three ways. One is when the complete needs of all workers involved in the productive process are not met. In this case prices are falsified in a downward direction. Another way that prices are kept artificially low is through externalizing certain costs and passing them on to other people, perhaps in developing countries or in future generations. These can be seen as debts that are foisted on parties who have not freely agreed to such arrangements. The third way is when unjustified costs are incorporated into the price, for example, whenever land or other means of production are treated as a commodity and are bought and sold for profit. What we are actually paying for in any purchase or leasing of land are rights, that is, the rights of access and use. Buying or renting land adds costs to any price calculation in the form of mortgages or rent payments that in turn offset mortgage payments. Rudolf Steiner makes an analogy between inflating currency and the inflationary effect of assigning land itself an economic value:

> Economically speaking, it makes no essential difference whether, for example, I issue money which has no foundation in reality but represents a mere increase in the amount of paper money, or whether I assign capital value to land. In both cases I am creating fictitious values. By inflating currency I increase prices of things numerically, but in the reality of the economic process, I effect absolutely nothing except a redistribution which may do immense harm to individuals. In like manner … capitalizing of land does harm to those who are involved in the economic process.[117]

The same insight can be applied to human-made means of production, which should also be viewed as community assets rather than private property, as already explained. Hence, buying and selling the means of production for profit also falsifies prices.

Associations and Meeting the Needs of Workers and Consumers

Both of Rudolf Steiner's formulations of true price explicitly address the needs of the workers. But they also assume that the legitimate needs of the consumers are being met in an efficient manner.

> Inasmuch as the purely economic value of a commodity (or service) expresses itself in money, which represents its equivalent value, this value will depend on the efficiency with which economic management runs things within the economic organism. ...The value of a commodity in money terms will thus express the fact that this commodity has been produced via the economic process in quantities which correspond to need.[118]

In the market economy there is seldom an occasion where the needs of producers (including the workers) and consumers are taken into consideration in open dialogue. In fact, producers and consumers are pitted against each other in the market. One seeks the highest possible price and the other seeks the lowest possible price, with little knowledge or concern for the other. We have seen that economic associations would provide the opportunity for all parties—producers, distributors, and consumers—to bring their needs to the table in full openness. Each party is then faced with the needs of the others. Thus, the agreed-upon price is established by the actual stakeholders through informed decision-making.[119] It is not imposed from outside by the state, nor simply left to the chances of the market and subject to the uncontrolled forces of supply and demand, nor is it determined through price-fixing by colluding parties to maximize profits. Through associations, prices can be determined through transparent accounting and informed analysis that reveal the complete costs and needs of each party involved.

Falsification of Prices through Usury, Speculation, and Deficit Spending

Prices can also be falsified through adding other unwarranted costs. When a person or institution gains wealth through speculation, or when governments authorize deficits with no intention of paying their debts, it has a general inflationary effect on prices, and consequently adds to the overall expenses and needs of workers.

Prices that Are True, Just, and Ethical

This cursory review of how the main principles of social threefolding and associative economics are operative in Rudolf Steiner's concept of a true price shows true prices as a reflection of a healthy dynamic among the three spheres of social life. A price is true when:

- Economically: products and services are produced in an efficient manner that meets real human needs, as determined by economic associations;

- Democratically: land, labor, and capital are no longer treated as commodities; workers receive a living income for themselves and their dependents; and the environment is protected from unjustified exploitation;

- Culturally: people are educated to develop their full creative capacities and to feel an ethical obligation to give back to the greater community whenever possible an equivalent value to what they have received from the labor of others.

Chapter 15

Egoism and Social Life

In any effort to understand and transform social life, it is essential to address the issue of egoism. We will first summarize the treatment of egoism as discussed in the preceding chapters and then add further thoughts.

Both the spiritual scientist Rudolf Steiner and the businessman and philanthropist Bill Gates agree that there are two fundamental forces in the human soul: egoism (self-interest) and love (caring for others). Rudolf Steiner calls the former forces "antisocial" and the latter "social." In his spiritually based worldview, the development of human individuality in evolution is seen as a necessary and appropriate preparation for our eventual conscious reuniting with our divine nature. A natural byproduct of this development of individualism is the increase of antisocial forces arising in the human soul. These need to be counterbalanced by the cultivation of social forces consisting of love and a concern for our fellow human beings. These can be fostered through education of children, inner exercises for adults, and appropriately formed societal organizations and institutions.

As we have seen, the Fundamental Social Law reveals egoism as the root cause of poverty, want, and suffering in the world. And conversely, the foundation or backbone of a healthy and prosperous social life is the ability to take increasing interest in each other.

For the development of social forces, an important inner quality to be fostered through education is the ability to think in pictures. Most education today encourages solely abstract thinking. Abstract thinking, especially when applied exclusively to social questions or issues, leaves the soul cold and indifferent to the thoughts, concerns, and plight of our fellow human beings. In contrast, imaginative thinking enables us to vividly picture or live into the situation of others.

Another quality or capacity needed for the development of social forces is the ability to listen with the soul, not only to the thoughts of the other person but also to the feelings that underlie the thoughts. Imaginative thinking and listening with the soul are important features of many new conversational techniques. The art and science of human conversation has become a significant component of social science research and practice over the last few decades. Several innovative approaches have been mentioned: Appreciative Learning, Goethean Conversation, World Café, Theory U, Non-violent Communication, and Focused Conversations.

The antisocial forces that have arisen through the inevitable strengthening of the I or ego need to be counterbalanced by the appropriate structures and dynamics of each of the three main spheres of social life—cultural, rights, and economic. We have seen how in an independent cultural life, the egoistic desire to develop one's capacities to the fullest degree possible is acknowledged and supported. However, in the same measure there needs to be a counterbalancing emphasis in education on developing social understanding, social sensitivity, and social skills. This dual emphasis results in what we have called ethical individualism: self-directed human beings whose individuality extends beyond personal ambition to work out of care and concern for others in social life, including the economy.

In an associative economy we have a dynamic interplay between egoism and altruism. The goal is not to simply overcome egoism but rather to address legitimate egoism in regard to the earthly needs of every person. All the legitimate requirements of consumers have their root in egoism. Rudolf Steiner expresses it this way:

And it is important that this fact should be properly understood. If it is understood, no one will be impelled to ask with regard to the economic life: How can we overcome egoism? but rather, How is it possible for altruism to meet the just demands of egoism?[120]

Two prerequisites for people to be able to work altruistically for others are: (1) that labor no longer be treated as a commodity, and (2) that they receive sufficient income to meet the needs of themselves and their dependents. Individuals who are continually preoccupied with the struggle for existence and who suffer the indignity of selling their labor for money can find little enthusiasm to work altruistically. True prices can never be obtained as long as workers are being exploited in such ways. The same is true for the environment. If out of egoism we exploit the environment to further economic growth and maximize profits without replenishing resources, then environmental costs are passed on to future generations and both current and future market prices are falsified.

In a true democratic political life, an equilibrium is found between egoism and interest in others.[121] Individuality is expressed democratically by having an equal say in the elective processes. The democratic process then turns individual decisions into majority rulings. Thus the individual yields to the decisions of the greater community. In addition, we as individuals expect equal protection under the law and trial by our peers if we are accused of transgressing the law. At the same time, we are expected to uphold equal protection and trial by jury for our fellow citizens out of concern for others.

We can see in this brief summary how a social organism based on threefold principles can help maintain a healthy balance of the two fundamental forces in the human soul—self-interest and concern for others.

PART FOUR:
FROM THOUGHTS TO MORAL ACTIONS

Chapter 16

An Associative Relations Audit as a Means of Transformation

Chapter 6 outlines how the main features of the modern market can be transformed. We will now focus on how small- to medium-size businesses and farms can help accelerate global transformation of the economy from the ground up, one person at a time, one farm at a time, one business at a time. We will here describe an Associative Relations Audit, a specialized method for assisting with this transformation.[122]

Associative economics is concerned with and depends on building and sustaining healthy relationships. Consequently, this audit focuses not on dollars and cents but on assessing the quality and types of relationships that are a part of a business or farm so as to promote team or group spirit, integrate idealism into daily operations, and enable an initiative to be more productive.

The Associative Relations Audit is a relatively simple assessment tool to provide specific information on a variety of important relationships. The managers of a farm or business can carry it out if they are familiar with associative economic principles; if not, a mentor can facilitate the process.

Maximizing efficiency and productivity, allocating resources to where they are most needed and can do the most good, establishing appropriate prices, ensuring a fair distribution of wealth, and achieving adequate prosperity for society all depend on healthy relationships with our fellow beings, the environment, and our own spiritual essence. Current business practices generally give these important relationships a much lower priority (if they are considered at all) than the so-called fiduciary duty of corporate management to maximize profits.

The Associative Relations Audit enables an organization to follow a process comparable to that of an individual taking stock of his or her life to establish personal goals and make resolutions for personal advancement. It begins with educating everyone involved about associative economics and the threefold nature of social life as an all-encompassing vision for a free, just, and prosperous society imbued with social and environmental responsibility. It then helps evaluate to what degree the organization's mission and core values are related to that vision. It concludes with identifying time-dated goals to improve various relationships.

The organization may work on only these goals or it may incorporate them into an overall strategic plan. The audit process can also lead to improving or establishing new relationships with other like-minded people, farms, and businesses, which, in turn, helps accelerate the overall growth of a new associative economy.

The Associative Relations Audit consists of evaluations of 13 types of relationships that may be part of an initiative.[123] The ideal situation is when the leadership works through the audit process together with as many management personnel and workers as possible. The more input that is gathered from all levels of the organization, the more valuable the results.

Aligning Mission, Vision, Goals, and Core Values

The Associative Relations Audit can be helpful in aligning mission, vision, goals, and core values in a very practical way, whether or not they have been articulated in written statements. A small-scale farmer may have a stronger relation on a day-to-day basis to goals and values in his or her own heart than someone working in a large organization has to a written mission statement, which may be filed in a desk or framed on a wall.

In any case, the first step is to determine whether the vision of an associative economy as described here finds a resonance with the organization's mission, vision, goals, and core values. If so, it may be worthwhile to consider doing the Audit.

Thirteen Types of Relations and Goals for Improving Quality of Relations

The 13 possible types of relationships that follow are not meant to be definitive but rather to provide a good basis for the assessment of vital relationships.[124] Not all the relationships listed may be applicable for a given endeavor. The types of relationships that are actually assessed will depend to some degree on the form of ownership and size of the farm or business. The main questions to be addressed for each type of relationship are: (1) What further steps within my initiative can I make toward the ideals and goals of an associative economy, and (2) What time-dated goals can I commit to?

All individuals and groups are in a continual process of reaching toward their full potential. Working toward specific goals is what matters, not some abstract ideal of perfection. We need to focus on becoming something—evolving, striving, even struggling—not being something or having become something. Furthermore, outer life continually changes, and consequently the need to assess relationships and make appropriate changes is ongoing.

(1) Relations with your customers, consumers, users of your product or service

Goals: As much as possible develop collaborative relations; create ongoing opportunities to dialogue and share the perspectives and the situations of both parties—provider and consumer. Get to know your customers. Enable your customers to know you. Be open about your needs. Take a genuine interest in their needs.

(2) Relations with your suppliers

Goals: Same as (1).

(3) Relations with like producers/service providers

Goals: Seek ways to collaborate with your peers, not compete. Through collaboration seek to do what you alone cannot do and to advance social well-being. Use combined resources for mutual benefit and to provide more, better, and/or more efficient services.

(4) **Relations of managers and workers to the spirit or the being of the farm or business**

Goals: Develop and maintain an ongoing educational process for all workers and managers to foster an understanding and appreciation of the organization's spiritual mission, core values, vision, and goals and how these each relate to day-to-day operations. Create opportunities for sharing experiences, knowledge, insights, and successes in the workplace. Encourage financial literacy and understanding of the business's finances and personnel policies.

(5) **Relations between management or owners and workers**

Goals: As far as possible, everyone who makes decisions should do so based on shared perspectives and informed insight. Maintain appropriate respect and civility. Paid labor—labor treated by management primarily as an expense that needs to be reduced to a minimum— needs to be overcome whenever possible.

(6) **Relations between managers**

Goals: Spirit of cooperation and collaboration. Maintain alignment with organization mission and vision.

(7) **Relations between management and investors and/or board members (as applies)**

Goals: Management should seek investors who share its mission and vision. Avoid investors who seek only money. Enable investors to know what they are supporting and its social significance. Keep investors informed of developments. Management, investors, and board members need to share a common mission and vision and work toward common goals.

(8) **Relations to the means of production**

Goals: Means of production should no longer be viewed as a commodity to be sold or used for personal profit. Seek legal forms by which the means of production are decommodified. The means of production need to be understood as a community asset that is made available to capable people who provide goods and/or services that meet community needs.

(9) Relations to the proceeds of an organization

Goals: Establish a fair and inclusive method of distributing proceeds. Establish a living wage and fair income range suitable for the locale.

(10) Relations to the natural and human-made environments

Goals: Not only minimize negative impact of the operations on nature but also improve upon the quality and appearance of the work environment and surroundings.[125] Bring artistic beauty to the workplace. Maintain order in all workspaces and penetrate them with consciousness. Everything and every activity should have an appropriate place. Establish environmentally-friendly policies regarding:

a) Types of energy sources;

b) Conservation, reuse, and recycling of resources;

c) Enhancement or improvement of the natural surroundings and the aesthetics of the human-made environments.

(11) Relations to machines and technology

Goals: Enable workers to understand how all machines and technological devices in the work place function. Develop a work culture in which machines serve the worker rather than the worker serving the machines.

(12) Relations to local cultural, charitable, and volunteer organizations

Goals: The organization, business, or farm should support education, research, and community aid activities that are in harmony with its mission, its community responsibilities, and the vision of an associative economy. Support local community volunteer agencies such as fire departments and ambulance squads.

(13) Relations of management and workers to spiritual development

Goals: To continually improve the character and capacities of all workers and management to be servant leaders in the enterprise and the community. To provide during work time opportunities for workers and management to engage in ongoing education in the fields of work and human and social development. Provide opportunities for and guidance in inner exercises that encourage the development of greater social and ethical capacities. Increased responsibility must go hand in hand with enhanced moral character. Every co-worker should be encouraged to be a leader or innovator in support of the spiritual mission and goals of the organization. The transformation of an organization and the larger economy needs to be accompanied, if not preceded, by individual soul transformation.

How to Conduct the Audit
Step One: Education

Participants in the audit process should familiarize themselves with the Fundamental Social Law, the threefold social organism, and associative economics. The preceding chapters in this book, other written material (referenced in endnotes), and knowledgeable mentors are possible sources for this preparation.

Step Two: Identify Harmony and Disharmony with Each Goal

For each type of relationship listed, identify operational activities, ownership forms, social dynamics, and policies in your business or farm that are in harmony with the stated goals, and those that are in opposition to them. (For new endeavors, think about goals that can be practically incorporated at the outset.)

Step Three: Prioritize and Implement Changes

Make a list of steps the organization could take toward realizing the intended goals. For example, steps in the direction of:

- enhancing relationships that already to some degree work in harmony with the goals,
- eliminating practices that inhibit healthy relationships, and
- establishing completely new activities or policies to support important relationships.

Prioritize these further steps for each relationship according to short-term and long-term goals, mindful of cost and time constraints or other factors.

When prioritizing goals it is important to remember that achieving the right dynamic balance is vital to every living organism. Just as a person who is a genius in one aspect of life may be ineffective in another, likewise a farm or business organism may be quite strong in some relationships but weak in others. This imbalance may have a crippling effect on the whole enterprise, and will most likely also show up in a financial audit.

Step Four: Set Goals and Monitor Progress

Choose the top priorities for improving each type of relationship according to the organization's means and needs. Then develop a plan that includes: time-dated goals, allocation of time and financial resources, assignments for people who are responsible for achieving the goals, and a method for monitoring progress. Do not hesitate to acknowledge that for the time being it may not be possible to make improvements in certain relationships owing to challenging outer circumstances or limited resources.

Two sayings attributed to Saint Francis of Assisi can provide some guidance for prioritizing goals and planning for their implementation:

Lord, grant me the serenity to accept the things I cannot change, the courage to change the things I can, and the wisdom to know the difference.

Start by doing what's necessary; then do what's possible; and suddenly you are doing the impossible.

Concluding Thoughts on the Associative Relations Audit

The Associative Relations Audit process can enable us to shape an initiative or enterprise from within. In so doing, an organization's strengths and weaknesses can be compared to the main features of an associative economy, and a strategic plan can be developed.

The Audit can also provide an opportunity for team-building, through which all participants contribute to identifying and prioritizing goals for the endeavor. And strategically, the Audit can be a useful tool for accelerating the transformation of the modern market into an associative economy at a local level.

Chapter 17

National Leverage Points

While it may be heartening to observe the proliferation of alternative economic and social initiatives emerging world-wide, some of which are referred to in previous chapters, there are three major institutions that have impeded and will continue to impede any significant change in the more troublesome aspects of the modern market economy. They are: (1) political interest groups, (2) the current political party system, and (3) government control and funding of education. Nothing less than a major grassroots political movement will be needed to counter and replace each of these institutions. Relentless pressure and strategic planning by organized citizenry are required if we are to hope for significant change in this regard.[126]

Interest Groups of All Sorts

There is no lack of statistics documenting the flow of money from tens of thousands of interest groups at the state and federal levels aimed at influencing elections and legislation. The federal government alone had 13,746 active registered interest groups that spent $3.49 billion lobbying elected officials on behalf of their agendas. Industrial interest groups play a major role in lobbying and electing officials as well. For example, from 1990 to 2010 AT&T contributed over $45 million to candidates, 45 percent to Democrats and 55 percent to Republicans. Individual candidates show no restraint in collecting funds from as many industries as possible. Chuck Schumer (D-NY), for instance, collected over $100 million from 12 of the 50 top U.S.

industries contributing to the 11th Congress during the 2009–2010 election cycle.[127] This flow of money has nothing to do with the democratic principles of individual equality and majority rule. Rather, such dynamics are better called "interest group pluralism," clearly a degenerate form of democracy that is determined by concentrations of money and power.

As is explained in Chapter 4, one of the main causes of social illness in our times is the domination of economic life over politics. It is hardly imaginable that we as a society can make any significant social change without making a greater effort to establish a right balance of power and jurisdiction between business and democracy. Robert Reich, former Secretary of Labor under President Bill Clinton, asserts in his recent book, *Supercapitalism*, that this is the single most important social task: "Keeping supercapitalism from spilling over into democracy is the only constructive agenda for change. All else, as I shall make clear [in this book], is frolic and detour."[128] We should, however, not limit our attention to neutralizing business and industrial interest groups in order to restore a balance between industry and labor unions. The arena of politicking interest groups is rot at the core of our democracy. One obvious area to begin this transformative process would be a stronger grassroots effort to reform campaign financing.

The Political Party System

Our current political party system consists of two major parties that are intractable opponents; because their oppositional stances keep them alive and active they are indispensable to each other. However, in regard to major issues like education reform, corporate bailouts, and foreign war policy, there is little operative difference between the Democratic and Republican parties. The differences in the so-called left- and right-wing tendencies of each of the parties are similar to the differences of a ship tacking to left and to right: a planned alternating movement in two seemingly opposed directions that ultimately results in moving forward in one common direction. This analogy holds whether there are only two major parties, as in the United

States Congress, or a host of parties collectively exhibiting two dominant tendencies, as is the case in many European Parliaments.

Interest groups fit into political parties like a hand in a glove. Political parties and their candidates are a thin flexible covering for interest groups to secure favorable legislation. Election campaigns have become an entertainment farce with as much credibility as so-called professional wrestling. Lying, deception, scripted speeches, personal attacks, unkept campaign promises, back door deals, and mass hysteria at conventions are all commonplace and supported by the parties. Through political parties the modern democratic process has degenerated into a display of some of the lowest forms of human instincts.

There is very little room to elect officials or pass legislation without being subject to the political party system. Write-in ballots and referenda are examples of the limited ways at a state or federal level, while the traditional New England town meetings are one of the few additional examples on a local level. These non-party options need to be greatly expanded. Within these non-party forms and processes, new ways of conversing need to be practiced to arrive at decisions that engender trust, respect, and inspired thoughts. Some of the techniques already referred to, such as World Café, Goethean Conversation, and Non-Violent Communication, can be drawn upon.

The development of a grassroots movement to rebuild our democracy without political parties would undoubtedly require a research and public education phase first. This would include a thorough analysis of the political party system and research into alternative election and legislation processes that are not encumbered by political parties. This phase could be followed by regional conversations dedicated to developing new ideas for restoring our democracy. Using the findings of such research, a strategic plan can then be developed for a grassroots political movement to effect the transformation.

Government-Run and Government-Financed Education

Reform of government-run and government-financed elementary and secondary schooling is subject to two powerful interest groups devoted to an agenda of self-preservation and profit. The first is big business, represented by such organizations as the National Business Roundtable (BRT), an association of CEOs of leading U.S. companies with nearly $6 trillion in annual revenues. Their main goal is to advocate for policies that foster vigorous economic growth and a dynamic global economy. The BRT has been a major architect in government education reform efforts at the state and federal levels for about two decades. While big business has shown support for parental choice in education, the proposals they currently advocate are based primarily on perpetuating the market economy and what is deemed good for economic growth, to the detriment of a well-balanced education. Moreover, their advocacy entails the use of stifling curriculum standards and the overuse of standardized tests.

The second major influence on education is teachers unions under the umbrellas of the National Education Association and the American Federation of Teachers. They are the single most powerful force opposing parental choice in education, especially if it involves faith-based and independent private schools. In recent years they have opposed every school choice proposal in the U.S. because any legislation that would expand the financial ability of parents to choose schools, especially private and charter schools, which are traditionally resistant to labor unions, will inevitably reduce the ranks and financial base of the teachers unions.

These two—big business and teachers unions—are the major interest groups who use the government to promote their agendas in education reform through lobbying and funding election campaigns. A variety of other groups likewise seek to influence government education, such as government school associations (school boards, principals, and teachers) and the textbook, computer, food, and student testing industries. With all of these vying and sometimes overlapping interests exerting influence on legislatures across the nation, there is little room for real education reform based on what children really need for their development.

For these and other reasons mentioned earlier, it is imperative that we progress toward a more diverse educational system funded directly by individuals and businesses—a system based on local control, parental choice, and diversity in educational options. The focus of education needs to be on the children and what they require to become independent, capable, socially responsible human beings who are equipped to bring their creative talents to life's tasks and challenges. Educators need to have an open and receptive eye to the future and what each generation has to offer to the furtherance of human civilization. They should not be limited to preserving the interests of certain powerful groups. In short, efforts to renew democracy and build an environmentally friendly, socially responsible, and vibrant economy need to be linked to a citizen-based social movement that advocates universal school choice.

Chapter 18

Local Leverage Points

In conclusion, I would like to share a few thoughts and suggestions on how to accelerate the transformation of the market economy toward a more associative economy on a local level.

Create Convergences of Like-Minded People and Organizations

Over the last few decades many alternative movements have arisen, each trying to address some specific aspect of social injustice or environmental exploitation. The time has come for individuals in such movements to meet and work together as much as possible. This is essential for the timely development of sufficient force to change the existing economic system. The many possibilities for working together include green expositions and festivals, multi-organizational World Café conversations, study and research groups, and collaborative projects.

Land Donations

One of the major ways that prices are falsified is the treating of land as a commodity that is bought and sold for personal or business profit. Escalated real estate prices are particularly challenging for small local and start-up businesses and not-for-profit enterprises. Monetary donations or direct land donations to land trusts are effective ways to remove land from the commodity market and make it available for the community (see next section).

Clustering Like-Minded People and Organizations

The development of like-minded organizations can be supported on a local level by bringing them together in close physical proximity. One way to do this is to establish nonprofit multi-tenant centers that provide affordable spaces for not-for-profits and/or local businesses. The Nonprofit Centers Network is set up to assist in the creation and operation of such centers.[129] They have over 200 centers listed on their web site, either in the planning stages or already in operation.

Community Land Trusts are another way to facilitate the clustering of like-minded mutually supportive enterprises. Originally, community land trusts were established to provide for affordable housing. But land trusts can provide for multifaceted communities, including farms, retail stores, light industry, and schools. Green retail and industrial centers that cluster like-minded local and regional businesses offer a way to further increase mutual support and market visibility.

Complementary Currencies and Transparent Accounting

Real transformation of economic life cannot happen without the transformation of money itself. Money has come to be perceived and treated as a thing unto itself, a precious commodity to be traded, hoarded, and speculated on. Whoever possesses it and controls its flow has power over others—the power to command the labor of others without equitable reciprocation.

Money once again must be understood and used for what it actually is: a representation of values, a transparent bookkeeping or accounting system of values being actually created, traded, lent, or given away. We need to learn anew how to create and use money in a conscious way on a local level. In addition to its other benefits, the complementary currency movement provides a way for people to re-educate themselves regarding money's role in society, its meaning and power.[130]

Conduct an Associative Relations Audit for Your Organization

Individual businesses can deepen their understanding of associative economics and progress toward transformation by working with the Associative Relations Audit as recommended in Chapter 16.

Focus on Rebuilding the Local Food Economy on an Associative Basis

Economic life arose and has evolved from agriculture and work on the land. Food production, distribution, and consumption are prime areas to start building a new associative economy at local and regional levels. CSA farms and Buy Local Campaigns are good ways to begin.[131] After several local CSAs are established, consumers can then associate together and extend their vision of a local food economy beyond a single farm, as described in Chapter 8 on trans-sector associations.

Harness the Power of Art for Social Renewal

Art has always had the potential to develop inner or spiritual qualities important for social life, including social sensitivity and creative thinking. Art also can be a powerful medium for conveying important spiritual and social ideals. The ideals of the Fundamental Social Law, social threefolding, and associative economics could be expressed through poetry, drama, music, painting, sculpture, documentaries, and so on. One of Europe's most influential modern artists, Joseph Beuys (1921–1986), dedicated his later years to promoting Steiner's social ideas.

Capitalization Fund for Local Businesses

Rebuilding local food economies will require new organizations and methods to capitalize local and regional enterprises. The Slow Money Alliance is one effort in this direction that supports local food systems. RSF Social Finance also fosters the creation of local capitalization funds for socially and environmentally responsible enterprises.[132]

Chapter 19

Aligning Pedagogy and Finance in a Waldorf School

In deference to the fact that this book is published by the Association of Waldorf Schools of North America, I am including this short essay specifically for administrators and board members of independent Waldorf schools. It suggests ways to begin thinking about and implementing the principles of economic associations within the financial structures of their schools.

One of the great challenges to sustainability facing independent Waldorf schools is how to view and work with finances. Many people devoted to Waldorf education are asking the question: Is it possible for school leadership to work in the fiscal realm by drawing on the same profound soul-spiritual values, view of the human being, and view of the world that the teachers draw on in the classroom? Apart from its importance for the fiscal stability of schools, this question is relevant for the pedagogy because the children will sense the discrepancies in the school life between what they are taught and what they hear and see their teachers, school staff, and their parents saying and doing.[133]

This essay explores some specific ways to approach two related aspects of a school's finances—budgeting and tuition setting—to make them more consistent with the spiritual foundation of the curriculum as well as the social understanding, sensitivity, and skills that the students have the opportunity to learn.[134]

Historical Background and Modern Context

The Waldorf school movement, based on the social and spiritual insights of Rudolf Steiner, arose out of earlier efforts to implement the ideals of a threefold social organism. These ideals call for freedom in cultural life, including education; equality in politics; and fellowship in an associative economy. Associative economics is rooted in the principles of cooperation and concern for others rather than competition and self-interested behavior, which are the main principles undergirding the modern market economy. Steiner maintained that in order to have a healthy impact, economic decisions need to be determined by associations of people involved in the economic processes, including production, distribution, and consumption. Open dialogue and transparency are essential features of these associations. Decisions regarding pricing, quantities, and quality standards are healthy to the extent that they draw upon the insights and intelligence of the participants rather than being left to the forces of supply and demand guided by the intelligence of a free market or the government. Elements of this approach can be found in many alternative social movements today, including fair trade, community supported agriculture, community land trusts, and social finance.

The examples of the associative approach to tuition and finances used here are drawn from the work of the Institute for Social Renewal, particularly the Accessible to All tuition approach first developed by Bob Monsen and Mary Roscoe at the Waldorf School of the Peninsula in 1993.[135]

Creating a Budget: Inflated Income vs. Anticipated Income

For independent schools, the typical approach to budget creation is to assume at the outset that all families will pay full tuition. The amount of tuition assistance to be offered is based on a certain percentage of the total tuition income (10 percent to 12 percent is often recommended).[136] For example, if there are 100 children in the school and the tuition is set at $10,000 per child, the overall starting income figure for the budget is

Polarities in Approaches to Tuition Determination in Independent Waldorf Schools

Tuition Approach	World View	Social Gesture	Initial Budgeted Income	Budget & Tuition Setting Process	Tuition Assistance/ Reduction
Market Perspective	Self-interest, competition /Spiritual subsidiary to finances	Closed process/ Education viewed as a commodity	Based on all families paying full tuition	Limited review prior to setting the budget and tuition	Impersonal, formulaic third-party review and determination
Associative Perspective	Cooperation and concern for others/ Finances an extension of spiritual	Inclusive, open process /Education viewed as soul-spiritual activity	Based on anticipated income from parents[137]	Inclusive process prior to setting budget and tuition	Face to face personal conversations between families and school representatives

Illustration 6

$1 million. Let's assume that the amount of tuition assistance to be awarded is set at 12 percent of full tuition income. The school would then posit that it has $120,000 available for tuition assistance. In addition to this formulaic approach, many schools set a maximum percentage of how much tuition assistance a family is eligible to receive. This is typically set at 50 percent, which in this example is $5,000.

When the initial budget is based on everyone's paying full tuition, it is inevitable that any family which cannot do so is viewed financially as having a negative effect on the school's budget, and consequently as someone who must be sustained by those paying full tuition and/or donors. The resulting division in the parent body—whether it be psychological, class-based, or lifestyle choices—is just one unhealthy outcome of this approach.

In order to avoid this problem and begin to work more associatively, a school can change the way it creates a budget by using projected numbers from the outset, that is, by estimating the actual estimated revenue, including tuition from all families for the coming year.

A budget that is based on projected income from all families supports the idea that every family's tuition contribution is appreciated and helps meet the overall budget. The school would be worse off financially, and in many cases pedagogically and socially, if families who can pay only partial tuition were not in the school. If you took the income out of the budget from families who pay a partial tuition, the tuition would be even higher for the full paying families, at least until the school reaches the point of full enrollment. It is likely that this more associative way of working will have a positive effect on the school's finances, the social relations of the parents, and the social dynamics in the classroom as well.

The Budget and Tuition Setting Process

Often the budget and tuition setting process is a closed internal process until it is finalized. This excludes the majority of the people who will be most affected by the new budget and tuition rates: the parents, and sometimes even the teachers. The budget and tuition are then presented to the school community in a finished form. A more inclusive associative approach is possible, as follows.

The school trustees or an appointed committee begin the budget process by reviewing:

1. the current income and expense report, cash flow status, and budget projections for the current year with the business manager.
2. income levels of teachers and staff in relation to their financial needs.
3. program, facility, and staffing needs with the teachers and administration.
4. current enrollment status and projections for next year with the enrollment coordinator.
5. the affordability of any possible tuition rate increases for the current parents, initially with a small sampling of parents, business manager, and tuition adjustment committee.
6. the anticipated donation income with the development director or development committee.

Based on these initial findings, the committee then drafts a preliminary balanced budget for the following school year with proposed tuition rates. The next step is for the school to have conversations about the proposed budget and tuition (if necessary, providing more than one option), one with the full faculty and staff and one with the parent body and possibly selected donors. The parent conversations could be done at an all-school meeting or in smaller focus groups.

The more the school understands the effects of the proposed budget on parents and teachers, and the more the parent body has the opportunity to understand the reality behind the numbers on the school's side, the more likely that annual budgets will be supported. Such mutual understanding also creates an optimal social climate for inspired creative ideas to arise for how to increase the overall support of the school. This can help counter the poverty mentality that often afflicts schools.

Obviously, it is much better to address areas of possible tension openly, prior to the budget being set, rather than have lingering dissatisfaction and gossip undermine the social climate of the school afterward. This open and informed dialogue prior to making a final decision regarding finances is a fundamental principle of working associatively.

Once the budget and tuition are set, it is then possible to work in a healthy way with individual families who cannot pay the full tuition and for the school development committee to plan how to achieve the annual appeal goal.

Tuition Reduction Process

Most schools use a third party evaluation service to analyze the financial circumstances of families who can't afford full tuition and to determine what they can afford to pay. Some use the third party's determination as the final say in what a family must pay. Others use it as one of several determining factors. In these cases, there is usually no in-person meeting of the school with the applicant family unless the school provides for a conversation in an appeal process. Thus, in-person conversations are at best a last resort measure. In a more associative approach, the tuition adjustment conversation is central to the whole process. The goal of these conversations between families and school representatives is to arrive at a mutually agreed upon tuition amount after each party is fully informed about the other's circumstances.[138] During the conversation, the representatives of the school begin by acknowledging and expressing appreciation for the family's participation in the school community. They then share the school budget and financial report along with the mission and vision of the school. This could include a multi-year strategic plan. In essence, they are painting a picture of the overall financial, pedagogical, and social state of the school. Once that is completed, the financial situation of the family is reviewed in relation to its capacity to support the school's current and future needs. This support can and hopefully will go beyond simply paying tuition. If donations of money are not possible, the family could be helpful in other ways, for example, in advertising the school's open houses in their neighborhood. The idea is to create a conversational mood that encourages trust and inspired ideas to arise rather than a mood of the competitive market in which the family's goal is to pay as little as possible to the school and the school's goal is to extract as much money from the family as possible. The final decision of the amount of tuition is mutually determined by both the family and the school representatives. The center and focus of the conversation should be how the best education and greatest well-being of the children in the school can be achieved through cooperation between the families and the school.

The success of working in this associative way hinges on the ability of the school conversationalists first of all to create a mood of openness and trust, and then to paint a sufficiently clear picture of the school's finances, mission, and values so that parents will freely contribute as much as they can out of appreciation and insight. It is essential that the school representatives take into consideration the family's situation while being equally responsible for the financial goals of the school. Too much sympathy for the family's situation will result in less than optimum support for the school. Inflexibility regarding the school finances can undermine the conversation and elicit an adversarial attitude from the family.

Approximately 25 Waldorf schools in the U.S. are working or have worked with this associative approach to tuition adjustment, with admittedly varying degrees of success both financially and socially. The primary factor in success is the ability of the school conversationalists to work in the manner described and to continually maintain these practices.[139] Working in this more associative way is challenging because it is contrary to the normal way of operating in the competitive capitalistic market, which is based on maximizing self-interest and competition. Nonetheless, for parents, teachers, staff, and board members to make the requisite effort to align the finances with the educational mission of the school is well worthwhile and can only have a beneficial effect on the whole school community.[140]

Chapter 20

From Big Thinking and Small Steps to Systemic Change

The question may legitimately be asked whether the relatively small incremental steps for implementing the radical ideas presented in this book—even if they lend credibility to the ideas and are effective on a local level—will have any measurable effect in relation to the greater economic life and the world of international finance.

In answering, we need first to recognize that while many steps taken toward a freer democratic society and associative economy are small, their sheer numbers indicate a massive, emerging elemental force. Paul Hawken's research has identified hundreds of thousands of initiatives characterized by unity of thought—social justice, cultural tolerance, and environmental responsibility. This constitutes a powerful force that has not by any measure reached its full size and scope. The infusing of the social organism with life-enhancing social initiatives, if only in homeopathic doses, is a strong indication of healthier social times to come.

Although it is true that the more these separate initiatives and movements can forge alliances and merge their efforts, the greater will be the scope and force of their effects, we should not be so naïve as to think that there will be little resistance to the transformation of the economy, our government, and the educational system. The more these social ideas gain public notice and favor, the more vigorously they will be fought by those who benefit from the current arrangements even though these arrangements may be detrimental to other people and the environment. We should not shirk from such challenges, for nothing less than the future of human civilization is at stake. Those with interests to protect have wealth and power and no inhibitions against using them politically to safeguard and promote their interests. We can be inspired, empowered, and guided by the ideals of justice and concern for all people. Let us be confident that no effort on behalf of others will be lost for the progress of humanity.

We have reached a turning point in human history: we can no longer pursue the destructive path of egoism and ruthless economic competition without causing irreparable harm to our planet and future civilizations. We now need to choose love and care for others over the pursuit of personal gain in our economic life and in so doing link ourselves with others the world over who are making the same choice.

Endnotes

1. Steiner, Rudolf. *Knowledge of the Higher Worlds and Its Attainment*, New York: Anthroposophic Press, 1975, p. 1.

2. Examples of people whose work in various fields is influenced by the social ideas of Rudolf Steiner are: Trauger Groh, Community Supported Agriculture; Robert Swann, Community Land Trusts and complementary currencies; Paul Mackay, ethical banking; Sigfried Finser, social finance; Christian Gelleri, complementary currencies; Claus Sproll, Green Party; Nicanor Perlas, Philippines politics; Ehrenfried Pfeiffer, sustainable agriculture; Paul Scharff, complementary medicine; Patrice Maynard, educational freedom.

3. Karp, Robert. *Toward an Associative Economy in the Sustainable Food and Farming Movement*, Milwaukee, WI: New Spirit Ventures, 2007, p. 9; Korten, David. "Renewing the American Experiment," http://www.tikkun.org/article.php/DavidC.Korten and http://www.developmentforum.org/Experiment.

4. As quoted in an e-mail communication June 11, 2010, with the subject line "An Economy Expressing our Highest Ideals." For more information see: http://www.neweconomicsinstitute.org.

5. Steiner, Rudolf. *Intuitive Thinking as a Spiritual Path: A Philosophy of Freedom*, Hudson, NY: Anthroposophic Press, 1995. Other English translations have appeared under the titles *The Philosophy of Freedom* and *The Philosophy of Spiritual Activity*.

6. Now published as a booklet *Anthroposophy and the Social Question*, Chestnut Ridge, NY: Mercury Press, 2003.

7. His various characterizations of the Fundamental Social Law can be found in the booklet *Selected Passages from Writings and Lectures Related to the Fundamental Social Law*, comp. Gary Lamb, Loma Mar, CA: Institute for Social Renewal, 2006.

8. Rudolf Steiner has characterized Anthroposophy as a path of knowledge leading from the spirit of the human being to the spirit in the universe.

9.   Rudolf Steiner's first written reference to the threefold nature of the human physical organism was in 1917. It can be found in addendum 6 in *Riddles of the Soul*, Spring Valley, NY: Mercury Press, 1996. More recently, Dr. Johannes W. Rohen, an eminent author of anatomy books used in the medical field, who is familiar with Steiner's works, has written an excellent modern text on the threefold nature of the human organism, *Functional Morphology: The Dynamic Wholeness of the Human Organism*, Hillsdale, NY: Adonis Press, 2007.

10. These memoranda can be found in Steiner, Rudolf. *Social and Political Science*, Forest Row, England: Sophia Books, 2003.

11. The organization was called The Union for the Threefold Order and was founded on April 22, 1919. It is referenced in Steiner, Rudolf. *Education as a Force for Social Change,* Hudson, NY: Anthroposophic Press, 1997, p. xxvi.

12. The appeal can be found in *Towards Social Renewal*, London: Rudolf Steiner Press, 1999, p. 121. The original German title of the book is *Die Kernpunkte der socialen Frage*; it has been published in English under other titles, including *The Threefold State*, *The Threefold Commonwealth*, and *The Threefold Social Order*.

13. For more on the social mission of Waldorf education see: Lamb, Gary. *The Social Mission of Waldorf Education*, Fair Oaks, CA: AWSNA Publications, 2004. The ideal of accessibility to all regardless of economic circumstances is particularly challenging for independent Waldorf schools in the United States, since they rely mainly on parent tuition for financial support.

14. There are currently two English translations of these lectures: *World Economy*, London: Rudolf Steiner Press, 1977, and *Economics: The World as One Economy*, Bristol, England: New Economy Publications, 1996. There will soon be a new American edition to be published by SteinerBooks, Great Barrington, MA.

15. The lectures on social threefolding can be found in *Rudolf Steiner Speaks to the British*, London: Rudolf Steiner Press, 1998, pt. 2, pp. 105–166.

16. "New Scheme of Social Organization: A Review by Raymond G. Fuller," *New York Times*, January 14, 1923, as quoted in Rudolf Steiner, "Threefold Social Organism, and Christianity," *American and British Newspaper and Journal Reviews*: 1923 and 1924, Loma Mar, CA: Institute for Social Renewal, 2006, p. 3.

17. "Rudolf Steiner: A Review by W.F. Lofthouse," *The London Quarterly Review 139* (January 1923): pp. 35–48, as quoted in Rudolf Steiner, *Threefold Social Organism, and Christianity*, American and British Newspaper and Journal Reviews: 1923 and 1924, Loma Mar, CA: Institute for Social Renewal, 2006, pp. 10–11.

18. Rudolf Steiner's *Conferences with the Teachers of the Waldorf School in Stuttgart, 1923–1924*, Forest Row, England: Steiner Schools Fellowship Publications, 1989, vol. 4: pp. 64–65. From a conference held on February 5, 1924.

19. Needleman, Jacob. *The American Soul: Recovering the Wisdom of the Founders*, New York: Tarcher/Putnam, 2002, p. 6.

20. Eisler, Riane. *The Real Wealth of Nations: Creating a Caring Economics*, San Francisco: Berrett-Koehler Publishers, 2007, p. 28.

21. Steiner, Rudolf. *Spiritual Science as a Foundation for Social Forms*, Hudson, NY: Anthroposophic Press, 1986, pp. 189–190.

22. Testimony by Alan Greenspan given on July 16, 2002, to the Senate Committee on Banking, Housing, and Urban Affairs and on July 17, 2002, to the House of Representatives Committee on Financial Services found at http://www.federalreserve.gov/boarddocs/hh/2002/july/testimony.html.

23. The term *alternative economics* has usually been limited to mean socialism as an alternative to capitalism. The term as used here goes beyond these two economic views.

24. Korten, David. *When Corporations Rule the World*, West Hartford, CT: Kumarian Press; San Francisco: Berrett-Koehler Publishers, 1995, pp. 325–326.

25. Rudolf Steiner's vast works include some 30 books and over 6,000 lectures and essays. For a substantial selection of his works in English, visit http://www.steinerbooks.org.

26. For a modern argument for a more caring economy see: Eisler, *Real Wealth of Nations*.

27. See: Steiner, Rudolf. *An Outline of Esoteric Science*, Great Barrington, MA: SteinerBooks, 1997.

28. For more on Waldorf education, biodynamic agriculture, and the Christian Community respectively visit http://www.whywaldorfworks. org; http://www.biodynamics.com; and http://www.thechristiancommunity.org.

29. Native Americans were, and still are to some degree, innately connected to the spiritual world through nature, certainly more so than the early Europeans who came to this continent. They experienced wind, rain, clouds, sun, moon, stars, and all species of animals as expressions and extensions of the Great Spirit. This was not an abstract thought for them but a daily experience that filled their souls and guided their actions.

30. This author recognizes that the democratic impulse was not universal but quite restricted in its origin and early stages of development, and that its fulfillment will not occur until equality is a universal principle not limited by gender, class, race, or beliefs.

31. Scharmer, C. Otto. *Theory U*, Cambridge, MA: Society for Organizational Learning, 2007, p. 95.

32. Korten, David. *The Great Turning: From Empire to Earth Community*, San Francisco: Berrett-Koehler Publishers; Bloomfield, CT: Kumarian Press, 2006, pp. 37–38. Korten is perhaps the most widely read economist associated with the modern alternative economics movement. In his book he refers to a threefold society: economic, political, and cultural. He characterizes the "Great Turning" as consisting of an economic turning, a political turning, and a cultural turning. When he outlines his strategy for working toward an "Earth Community," he refers to the dynamics of living economies, living politics, and living cultures.

33. Two modern works on social threefolding are: Large, Martin. *Common Wealth for a Free, Equal, Mutual and Sustainable Society*, Stroud, England: Hawthorne Press, 2010; and Perlas, Nicanor. *Shaping Globalization: Civil Society, Cultural Power, and Threefolding*, Quezon City, Philippines: Center for Alternative Development Initiatives and Global Network for Social Threefolding, 2000.

34. See note 9. Rohen's *Color Atlas of Anatomy*, Philadelphia: Lippincott Williams & Wilkins, 2006, is well known to many American medical students.

35. For a full explication of the relationship between these three bodily systems and the three spheres of social life see Steiner's *Towards Social Renewal*. The understanding of these three systems also plays an important diagnostic and treatment role in Anthroposophically-

extended medicine pioneered by Rudolf Steiner and Dr. Ita Wegman. See their book: *Extending Practical Medicine: Fundamental Principles Based on the Science of the Spirit*, London: Rudolf Steiner Press, 1996, or visit http://www.paam.net. In addition to the threefolding of the body referred to here, Rudolf Steiner also describes the threefold nature of the soul and spirit of the human being. The soul can be viewed as having three primary functions of thinking, feeling, and willing. And the spirit can be viewed in terms of three levels of thinking or cognitive activity: imagination, inspiration, and intuition. For more on the soul and spirit functions see: Steiner, Rudolf. *How to Know Higher Worlds: A Modern Path of Initiation*, Hudson, NY: Anthroposophic Press, 1994.

36. For an excellent analysis of how business and corporate interests dominate cultural and political life, see: Korten, *When Corporations Rule*.

37. Economically speaking these needs range from basic necessities of food, clothing, and shelter to the need to experience and participate in art and religion.

38. See, for example: Hawken, Paul. *Blessed Unrest: How the Largest Movement in the World Came into Being and Why No One Saw It Coming*, New York: Viking Press, 2007.

39. For more on associative economics see: Budd, Christopher, Ph.D. and Arthur Edwards, editors. *Associate! A Digest from the World of Economics*, http://www.cfae.biz/publications/.

40. A classic 19th century work on mutual aid is Kropotkin, Pyotr Alexeyevich. *Mutual Aid: A Factor in Human Evolution*, New York: Dover Books, 2006.

41. A reference often used in support of this viewpoint is Adam Smith's *The Wealth of Nations* originally published in 1776.

42. See: Steiner's *Selected Passages*.

43. One perspective in support of the principles of self-interest and competition in economic life is Friedman, Milton, *Capitalism and Freedom*, Chicago: University of Chicago Press, 2002. Another is the January 24, 2008, speech by Bill Gates at the Economic Forum in Davos, Switzerland, found at http://www.gatesfoundation.org/speeches-commentary/Pages/bill-gates-2008-world-economic-forum-creative-capitalism.aspx.

44. Korten, *Great Turning* and Hawken, *Blessed Unrest.*

45. Pink, Daniel. *Drive: The Surprising Truth of What Motivates Us*, New York: Riverhead Books, 2009, p. 204.

46. Pink, however, does not go quite as far as Steiner's picture of maximizing the well-being or wealth of a whole community. Pink describes how the motive of purpose is already expressing itself in three ways in businesses: "in goals that use profit to reach a purpose; in words that emphasize more than self-interest; and in policies that allow people to pursue purpose on their own terms." Pink conjectures that a "move to accompany profit maximization with purpose maximization has the potential to rejuvenate our businesses and remake our world." (208). However, from the standpoint of the Fundamental Social Law, it is a group of people united and motivated by a great purpose (the needs of others) that will yield the greatest well-being (profit, as one indicator) for a community. Nonetheless, Pink has uncovered important data on human motivation that in many ways supports Steiner's Fundamental Social Law.

47. While I have drawn significantly from Steiner's writings on the Fundamental Social Law, I am responsible for this characterization of the Law and the corollaries as presented here. This includes references to people and organizations after Steiner's time who I believe are working to some degree in harmony with the Law.

48. For research on the beneficial effects of sustainable agriculture on the environment visit Farmscape Ecology Program at: http://www.hawthornevalleyassociation.org.

49. Washington, Booker T. *Up from Slavery*, Pathfinder edition, New York: Bantam Books, 1967.

50. For more information on these respectively, visit http://www.appreciativeinquiry.case.edu; http://www.ica-usa.org; http://www.cnvc.org; http://www.ottoscharmer.com; and http://www.theworldcafe.com. For more on Goethean Conversation see: Spock, Marjorie. *Group Moral Artistry II: The Art of Goethean Conversation*, Spring Valley, NY: St. George Press, 1983.

51. Creative imagination is one of the core capacities that Waldorf education strives to develop in each student.

52. For examples of such inner exercises see: Steiner, Rudolf. *Social and Antisocial Forces*, Spring Valley, NY: Mercury Press, 2003.

53. This is one of the main features of a threefold social organism as described in Chapter 4.

54. Thoreau, Henry David. "Life Without Principle," in *Thoreau: Walden and Other Writings*, New York: Bantam Books, 1965, pp. 358–359.

55. See: Leitner, Bernard. *Community Currencies: A New Tool for the 21st Century* found at http://www.transaction.net/money.cc/ccol.html.

56. Gelleri, Christian. "Chiemgauer Regiomoney: Theory and Practice of a Local Currency," *International Journal of Community Currency Research*, *13* (2009): pp. 61–75, http://www.uea.ac.uk/env/ijccr/.

57. See Steiner, *World Economy*, lecture 2.

58. Examples of organizations in the United States working with Community Land Trusts are Equity Trust, Institute for Community Economics, E.F. Schumacher Society, and National Land Trust Network found respectively at http://www.equitytrust.org; http://www.iceclt.org; http://www.schumacher society.org; and http://www.cltnetwork.org.

59. See: http://www.newrules.org.

60. For more on principles in economics related to Rudolf Steiner's social ideas see: Spence, Michael. *After Capitalism*, found at http://www.socialrenewal.com/pdfs/After Capitalism 12-09.pdf and Herrmann-storfer, Udo. *Pseudo Market Economy*, found at http://www.threefolding.net/Pseudo_Market_Economy.pdf. These are important works that go into greater detail than the present book.

61. A materialistic view of the world represents physical matter as the only reality and claims that everything, including thought, feeling, mind, and will, can be explained in terms of matter and physical phenomena. This view can easily lead to an excessive self-interest and desire for money and possessions rather than ethical values.

62. See note 43.

63. Waldorf schools, for example, provide a more balanced approach to the study of economics.

64. Smith, Adam. *An Inquiry into the Nature and Causes of the Wealth of Nations*, Indianapolis: Liberty Fund, Inc., 1981.

65. Guth, Robert A. "Bill Gates Issues Call for Kinder Capitalism: A Man Once Fixated on Profit Now Urges Business to Aid the Poor," *Wall Street Journal*, January 24, 2008, A1, A15.

66. Friedman, *Capitalism and Freedom*, p. 133. There are multiple problems with this statement from an associative economics perspective, not the least of which is that corporate interests dictate the rules of the game to a large degree.

67. Smith, *Wealth of Nations*, p. 687. The full reference is: "All systems either of preference or of restraint, therefore, being thus completely taken away, the obvious and simple system of natural liberty establishes itself of its own accord. Every man, as long as he does not violate the laws of justice, is left perfectly free to pursue his own interest his own way, and to bring both his industry and capital into competition with those of any other man, or order of men. The sovereign is completely discharged from a duty, in the attempting to perform which he must always be exposed to innumerable delusions, and for the proper performance of which no human wisdom or knowledge could ever be sufficient; the duty of superintending the industry of private people, and of directing it towards the employments most suitable to the interest of the society."

68. Friedman, *Capitalism and Freedom*, p. 119.

69. Ibid., p. 120.

70. Smith, *Wealth of Nations*, p. 660. The full reference is: "Consumption is the sole end and purpose of all production; and the interest of the producer ought to be attended to, only so far as it may be necessary for promoting that of the consumer."

71. For more information on these cultural corporations that would administer capital see: Steiner, Rudolf. *The Social Future*, Hudson, NY: Anthroposophic Press, 1972, pp. 118–121. An important source of information on shared resources that should not be treated as private property or a commodity is the commons movement. See: http://www.environmentalcommons.org and http://www.onthecommons.org.

72. See references in note 58.

73. For more on the question of wealth that is in harmony with the thoughts presented here see: Korten, David. Agenda for a *New Economy: From Phantom Wealth to Real Wealth*, San Francisco: Berrett-Koehler Publishers, 2009.

74. See notes 43 and 65.

75. Steiner, *World Economy*, lecture 14.

76. Former Vice-President Al Gore, now an environmental activist, recently gave his perspective on the importance of each generation's rising to the challenges of the times in a speech given in Monterey, CA, March 2008, found at http://www.ted.com/talks/al_gore_s_new_thinking_on_the_climate_crisis.html. It is sometimes referred to as the "Generational Speech."

77. Tocqueville, Alexis de. *Democracy in America*, New York: Penguin Books, 1984, p. 201.

78. Needleman, *American Soul*, p. 61.

79. Tocqueville, *Democracy in America*, p. 200.

80. For more on community supported agriculture in the U.S. visit http://www.biodynamics.com and http://www.csacenter.org.

81. Live Power Community Farm, http://www.livepower.org. Please note that they use the term Community Sustained Agriculture rather than Community Supported Agriculture.

82. See: Lamb, Gary. "Community Supported Agriculture: Can It Become the Basis of a New Associative Economy?" *Biodynamics*, Kimberton, PA: Biodynamic Farming and Gardening Association, 196 (November/December 1994), pp. 8–15.

83. For example, Columbia County in the Hudson Valley Region in New York State has 15 CSA farm operations.

84. See the announcement by the Biodynamic Farming and Gardening Association on http://www.biodynamics.com of a new project to be launched in the U.S. "to help develop a new type of consumers' association designed to purchase and hold agricultural assets in order to support family farmers and protect consumer rights. The BDA will pilot the effort in Wisconsin and then look to share lessons from its use in other states."

85. For more information on Equal Exchange visit http://www.equal-exchange.com. Some people are critical of the Fair Trade movement seeing it as a short-term solution that does not address long-term systemic problems of farmers. Admittedly, Fair Trade by itself can effect

little change, but the more the movement can integrate into an overall approach of transforming economics that includes land and currency reform as described here, the more effective it will become.

86. For Remei's English language web site visit http://www.remei.ch/en/ unternehmen/daten-fakten.html.

87. Matthew 18:20.

88. Steiner, Rudolf. *The Influence of Spiritual Beings on Man*, New York: Anthroposophic Press, 1982, p. 156.

89. For more on the influence of big business on education reform in the U.S. see Lamb, *Social Mission of Waldorf Education*, pt. 2, pp. 51–83.

90. This survey was sponsored by the Foundation for Educational Choice, Indianapolis, IN, and conducted by Braun Research, Princeton, NJ, from July 26 to August 1, 2010. Sample sizes of registered voters were Alabama: 601; Arkansas: 603; Kansas: 602; Mississippi: 603; New Jersey: 602; New York: 603. Total number of samples was 3,614. Margin of error is ± 4.0 percentage points for each state sample; ± 1.6 percentage points for total sample.

91. These statements are my interpretation of social threefolding and should not be construed as an official statement by any Waldorf school or organization affiliated with Waldorf education.

92. These states have scholarship tax credits whereby individuals and/or businesses can obtain a tax credit if they contribute to a scholarship-granting organization or a school to help offset tuition. The following states have a personal educational expense tax credit: Illinois, Iowa, and Minnesota.

93. For more information see Lamb, *Independent Schools and School Choice Legislation*.

94. For more on educational assessments see: Zachos, Paul. "Discovering the True Nature of Educational Assessments," *Research Bulletin*, Wilton, NH: The Research Institute for Waldorf Education, vol. 9, no. 2 (2004): pp. 7–12.

95. See: Steiner, *World Economy*, lecture 11.

96. See: Ken Robinson's February 2006 speech on creativity at http://www.ted.com/talks/ken_robinson_says_schools_kill_creativity.html.

97. Steiner, Rudolf. *The New Spirituality*, Hudson, NY: Anthroposophic Press, 1988, p. 67.

98. See: Lamb, *Independent Schools and School Choice Legislation*.

99. This thought must be considered from the perspective of a threefold social organism as described here in which there are three equally important spheres—economic, political, and cultural (education). Such deliberations taking place under the current arrangements would simply be a power struggle between vying interest groups that control our political states.

100. Indiana has enacted an education tax credit program since this list was compiled.

101. The complete text can be found at http://www.cato.org/pub_display.php?pub_ed=8812.

102. Employing tax credits as a mechanism for funding education on a society-wide basis is definitely a step in the direction of creating direct funding streams for education that do not use public funds. However, this is still a manipulation of the tax code. A more positive step would be to develop society-wide funding systems for education and health care that are completely separate from the tax system. Technically speaking, contributions to schools and scholarship programs that are eligible for tax credits are distinct from government taxes and fees. But they are viewed as a legal variance or exemption from the normal workings of the taxation system. Direct financing of education ultimately needs to gain the status of a separate but equally valid method of supporting the education of children or citizens' health care. The changeover from a government-tax-funded system to a direct funding system that lies outside the purview of the state would probably mean that there would be two funding systems during the transition. The state's role in the direct funding system should be limited to determining: the amount of money to be transferred, who should pay, who is eligible to receive the funds, and ensuring that the funds are not misallocated.

103. See: http://www.slowmoneyalliance.org.

104. For more information visit respectively http://www.rsfsocialfinance.org; http://www.tblcapital.com; and http://www.sbk.com.

105. Greco, Thomas H., Jr. *The End of Money and the Future of Civilization*, White River Junction, VT: Chelsea Green Publishing, 2009, pp. 43–44.

106. From http://www.en.wikipedia.org/wiki/Bernard_Madoff.

107. Subprime mortgages are granted to borrowers whose credit history is not sufficient to qualify them for a conventional mortgage. They are offered favorable initial terms such as interest-only payments to entice them to take out a loan. However, when higher payments eventually come due, the borrowers are often forced to default. Derivatives are securities, or financial instruments, that get their value, or at least part of their value, from the value of another security, which is called the underlier. The underlier can come in many forms including commodities, mortgages, stocks, bonds, or currency. Derivatives offer the possibility of large rewards, but speculation in derivatives often assumes a great deal of risk.

108. More such individuals are mentioned in the recent book: Bloom, John. *The Genius of Money: Essays and Interviews: Reimagining the Financial World,* Great Barrington, MA: SteinerBooks, 2009. Another important work on money is: Finser, Siegfried E. *Money Can Heal: Evolving Our Consciousness,* Great Barrington, MA: SteinerBooks, 2006.

109. Riegel, E.C. "Breaking the English Tradition," edited and with comments by Thomas Greco, Jr., http://www.reinventingmoney.com/documents/BreakingEnglishTradition.pdf.

110. Steiner, Rudolf. *The Challenge of the Times*, Spring Valley, NY: Anthroposophic Press, 1941, pp. 55–57.

111. Steiner, *Towards Social Renewal*, p. 131.

112. Steiner, *World Economy*, p. 72.

113. Ibid.

114. Steiner, Rudolf. *Towards Social Renewal*, p. 131.

115. The first Benefit Corporation law was passed in April 2010, in Maryland, creating a new class of corporations required to create benefit for society as well as shareholders. Unlike traditional corporations, Benefit Corporations must by law create a material positive impact on society; consider how decisions affect employees, community and the environment; and publicly report their social and environmental performance using established third-party standards. For more on Benefit Corporations see: http://www.bcorporation.net.

116. Steiner, *World Economy*, p. 45.

117. Ibid., p. 67.

118. Steiner, *Towards Social Renewal*, pp. 94–95.

119. Michael Rozyne, co-director of the not-for-profit Red Tomato distribution company based in New England, has coined the phrases "dignity price" and "dignity deal." From the following description of the dignity deal, one can sense a relation between those terms and the principle of economic associations as expressed by Rudolf Steiner. "In terms of bringing fair trade home to our growers, we focus on a concept we call the dignity deal. A dignified deal starts in the winter when Red Tomato staff start a pricing conversation with the farmer to establish three numbers: last year's average, this year's ideal price, and the farmer's personal price floor—the lowest price the farmer can accept without losing both money and dignity." Source: http.//www.redtomato.org/fairtrade.php.

120. Steiner, *Social Future*, p. 133.

121. Here, of course, we are speaking in ideal terms in relation to democracy.

122. Although this audit process in theory can be applied to any type or size of business where there is good will on the part of management and owners, the possibility of working with it in any meaningful way within a publicly-traded stock company is greatly limited because the dynamics of such companies are inherently opposed to the Fundamental Social Law and the principles of associative economics.

123. The Associative Relations Audit was first presented at a workshop during a Biodynamic Farming and Gardening Association conference in August 2006 titled "Building Sustainable Communities: Agriculture as Foundation for Social Change." That year provided an account of another self-assessment tool with the publication of Cohen, Ben and Mal Warwick. *Values-Driven Business: How to Change the World, Make Money, and Have Fun*, San Francisco: Berrett-Koehler Publishers, 2006. The Associative Relations Audit covers more areas, whereas Cohen and Warwick's fine work goes into greater detail. The Associative Relations Audit evaluates social and environmental relations generally. It does not include farm-specific relationships associated with raising crops and animal husbandry, including relations to celestial bodies, and the animal, plant, and mineral kingdoms. This is a separate field of study addressed more fully in a biodynamic farming and gardening training. This training and the Audit overlap in some areas, however.

124. Other types of relationships may be added or may replace some listed here as associative economics and this new field of auditing evolve. Associative Relationship Audits that are specific to not-for-profit and cultural organizations such as schools and religious organizations, and

even political organizations, are certainly possible. Also, the goals that are connected to each type of relationship can and should be elaborated beyond what is provided here.

125. A principle of biodynamic agriculture is to not only minimize harm done to the environment but also restore and enhance fertility beyond the original state.

126. Examples of such groups worth studying for their organizational structure and techniques are Change.org, Organic Consumers Association, and MoveOn.org found respectively at http://www.change.org; http://www. organicconsumers.org; and http://www.moveon.org. Please note that by referring to these organizations I am not endorsing their political positions.

127. Center for Responsive Politics, http://www.opensecrets.org.

128. Reich, Robert B. *Supercapitalism: The Transformation of Business, Democracy, and Everyday Life*, New York: Vintage Books, 2008, p. 14.

129. See: http://www.nonprofitcenters.org.

130. See: http://www.complementarycurrencies.org and Hearn, Sarah. "Money: Reclaiming the Power to Create," http://www.thinkoutword.org.

131. For information on how to start a buy local campaign see: http://www. bigboxtoolkit.com/images/pdf/buylocal_howto.pdf.

132. See: http://www.slowmoneyalliance.org and http://www.rsfsocialfinance. org.

133. Many board members in Waldorf schools struggle with tuition setting because they live in the market framework conceptually and in their professions but wish with their hearts that it could be otherwise for their school.

134. This essay focuses primarily on tuition; fundraising and development could also be discussed from an associative perspective, which is not possible here owing to limitations of space.

135. For more information on the Accessible to All tuition approach see: http://www.socialrenewal.com.

136. The term *tuition assistance* may imply that a family is being helped because of some deficiency or inadequacy, in this case an insufficient

income. In their discussion of Accessible to All tuition, Monsen and Roscoe use the term *tuition adjustment*, which implies that tuition is adjusted according to a family's ability to contribute to the support of the school, thus diminishing the potential stigma of inadequacy.

137. Initially, this is based on statistics and experiences from previous fiscal years.

138. In order to help people overcome the idea that education is a commodity, Monsen also suggests using the phrase *conscious consensual contracted contributions* rather than the term *tuition*.

139. It should be clear that the effectiveness of this tuition approach can be hampered or even undermined by significant deficiencies in other areas, such as a lack of capable teachers or board members.

140. The Institute for Social Renewal offers training for school representatives who want to represent the school in tuition conversations. This includes the social and spiritual mission of Waldorf education and how to prepare for the conversations with the same reverent attentiveness practiced by teachers preparing to teach the children The Institute for Social Renewal also recommends that development conversations take place with families who can contribute the full suggested tuition. The focus of these conversations is the annual appeal rather than tuition. Ideally, a separate group of trained conversationalists working with the development office conducts these conversations.

Bibliography

Bloom, John. *The Genius of Money: Essays and Interviews: Reimagining the Financial World*, Great Barrington, MA: SteinerBooks, 2009.

Budd, Christopher, Ph.D. and Arthur Edwards, editors. *Associate! A Digest from the World of Economics*, http://www.cfae.biz/publications/.

Cohen, Ben and Mal Warwick. *Values-Driven Business: How to Change the World, Make Money, and Have Fun*, San Francisco: Berrett-Koehler Publishers, 2006.

Eisler, Riane. *The Real Wealth of Nations: Creating a Caring Economics*, San Francisco: Berrett-Koehler Publishers, 2007.

Finser, Siegfried E. *Money Can Heal: Evolving Our Consciousness*, Great Barrington, MA: SteinerBooks, 2006.

Friedman, Milton. *Capitalism and Freedom*, Chicago: University of Chicago Press, 2002.

Gates, Bill. "Bill Gates – 2008 World Economic Forum – Creative Capitalism," http://www.gatesfoundation.org/speeches-commentary/Pages/bill-gates-2008-world-economic-forum-creative-capitalism.aspx.

Gelleri, Christian. "Chiemgauer Regiomoney: Theory and Practice of a Local Currency," *International Journal of Community Currency Research 13* (2009), http://www.uea.ac.uk/env/ijccr/.

Gore, Al. "Al Gore's new thinking on the climate crisis," http://www.ted.com/talks/al_gore_s_new_thinking_on_the_climate_crisis.html.

Greco, Thomas H., Jr. *The End of Money and the Future of Civilization*, White River Junction, VT: Chelsea Green Publishing, 2009.

Guth, Robert A. "Bill Gates Issues Call for Kinder Capitalism: A Man Once Fixated on Profit Now Urges Business to Aid the Poor," *Wall Street Journal*, January 24, 2008, A1, A15.

Hawken, Paul. *Blessed Unrest: How the Largest Movement in the World Came into Being and Why No One Saw It Coming*, New York: Viking Press, 2007.

Hearn, Sarah. "Money: Reclaiming the Power to Create," http://www. thinkoutword.org/pdfs/money_Article.pdf.

Herrmannstorfer, Udo. *Pseudo Market Economy: Labour, Land, Capital and the Globalization of the Economy*, http://www.threefolding.net/Pseudo_ Market_Economy.pdf.

Institute for Social Renewal. Rudolf Steiner, *Threefold Social Organism, and Christianity*: American and British Newspaper and Journal Reviews: 1923 and 1924, Loma Mar, CA: Institute for Social Renewal, 2006.

Karp, Robert. *Toward an Associative Economy in the Sustainable Food and Farming Movement*, Milwaukee, WI: New Spirit Ventures, 2007.

Korten, David. *Agenda for a New Economy: From Phantom Wealth to Real Wealth*, San Francisco: Berrett-Koehler Publishers, 2009.

―――. *The Great Turning: From Empire to Earth Community*, San Francisco: Berrett-Koehler Publishers; Bloomfield, CT: Kumarian Press, 2006.

―――. "Renewing the American Experiment," http://www.tikkun.org/article. php/DavidC.Korten; http://www.developmentforum.org/Experiment.

―――. *When Corporations Rule the World*, West Hartford, CT: Kumarian Press; San Francisco: Berrett-Koehler Publishers, 1995.

Kropotkin, Pyotr Alexeyevich. *Mutual Aid: A Factor of Human Evolution*, New York: Dover Books, 2006.

Lamb, Gary. "Community Supported Agriculture: Can It Become the Basis of a New Associative Economy?" *Biodynamics* (Kimberton, PA: Biodynamic Farming and Gardening Association) 196 (November/December 1994): pp. 8–15.

―――. *The Social Mission of Waldorf Education*, Fair Oaks, CA: AWSNA Publications, 2004.

―――. "Your Child, Your Choice: If It Were Reality," in *Independent Schools and School Choice Legislation in the United States: Waldorf Perspectives* 2009, Minneapolis, MN: Association of Waldorf Schools in North America; Loma Mar, CA: Institute for Social Renewal, 2009, pp. 28–29.

Large, Martin. *Common Wealth for a Free, Equal, Mutual and Sustainable Society*, Stroud, England: Hawthorne Press, 2010.

Leitner, Bernard. *Community Currencies: A New Tool for the 21st Century*, http://www.transaction.net/money.cc/ccol.html.

Needleman, Jacob. *The American Soul: Recovering the Wisdom of the Founders*, New York: Tarcher/Putnam, 2002.

Perlas, Nicanor. *Shaping Globalization: Civil Society, Cultural Power, and Threefolding*, Quezon City, Philippines: Center for Alternative Development Initiatives and Global Network for Social Threefolding, 2000.

Pink, Daniel. *Drive: The Surprising Truth About What Motivates Us*, New York: Riverhead Books, 2009.

Reich, Robert B. *Supercapitalism: The Transformation of Business, Democracy, and Everyday Life*, New York: Vintage Books, 2008.

Riegel, E.C. "Breaking the English Tradition," edited and with comments by Thomas Greco, Jr., http://www.reinventingmoney.com/documents/BreakingEnglishTradition.pdf.

Robinson, Ken. "Ken Robinson says schools kill creativity," http://www.ted.com/talks/ken_robinson_says_schools_kill_creativity.html.

Rohen, Johannes W. *Color Atlas of Anatomy*, Philadelphia: Lippincott Williams & Wilkins, 2006.

————. *Functional Morphology: The Dynamic Wholeness of the Human Organism*, Hillsdale, NY: Adonis Press, 2007.

Schaeffer, Adam B. "Policy Analysis: The Public Education Tax Credit," http://www.cato.org/pub_display.php?pub_id=8812.

Scharmer, C. Otto. *Theory U: Leading from the Future as It Emerges*, Cambridge, MA: Society for Organizational Learning, 2007.

Smith, Adam. *An Inquiry into the Nature and Causes of the Wealth of Nations*, Indianapolis: Liberty Fund, Inc., 1981.

Spence, Michael. *After Capitalism*, http://www.socialrenewal.com/pdfs/After Capitalism 12-09.pdf.

Spock, Marjorie. *Group Moral Artistry II: The Art of Goethean Conversation*, Spring Valley, NY: St. George Press, 1983.

Steiner, Rudolf. *Anthroposophy and the Social Question*, Chestnut Ridge, NY: Mercury Press, 2003.

———. *The Challenge of the Times*, Spring Valley, NY: Anthroposophic Press, 1941.

———. *Economics: The World as One Economy*, Bristol, England: New Economy Publications, 1996. Also published as *World Economy*, London: Rudolf Steiner Press, 1977.

———. *Education as a Force for Social Change*, Hudson, NY: Anthroposophic Press, 1997.

———. *How to Know Higher Worlds: A Modern Path of Initiation*, Hudson, NY: Anthroposophic Press, 1994. Also published as *Knowledge of the Higher Worlds and Its Attainment*, New York: Anthroposophic Press, 1975.

———. *The Influence of Spiritual Beings on Man*, New York: Anthroposophic Press, 1982.

———. *Intuitive Thinking as a Spiritual Path: A Philosophy of Freedom*, Hudson, NY: Anthroposophic Press, 1995.

———. *Knowledge of the Higher Worlds and Its Attainment*, New York: Anthroposophic Press, 1975. Also published as *How to Know Higher Worlds: A Modern Path of Initiation*, Hudson, NY: Anthroposophic Press, 1994.

———. *The New Spirituality*, Hudson, NY: Anthroposophic Press, 1988.

———. *An Outline of Esoteric Science*, Great Barrington, MA: SteinerBooks, 1997.

———. *Riddles of the Soul*, Spring Valley, NY: Mercury Press, 1996.

———. *Rudolf Steiner Speaks to the British*, London: Rudolf Steiner Press, 1998.

———. *Rudolf Steiner's Conferences with the Teachers of the Waldorf School in Stuttgart, 1923–1924*, Forest Row, England: Steiner Schools Fellowship Publications, 1989.

————. *Selected Passages from Writings and Lectures Related to the Fundamental Social Law,* compiled by Gary Lamb, Loma Mar, CA: Institute for Social Renewal, 2006.

————. *Social and Antisocial Forces,* Spring Valley, NY: Mercury Press, 2003.

————. *Social and Political Science,* Forest Row, England: Sophia Books, 2003.

————. *The Social Future,* Hudson, NY: Anthroposophic Press, 1972.

————. *Spiritual Science as a Foundation for Social Forms,* Hudson, NY: Anthroposophic Press, 1986.

————. *Towards Social Renewal,* London: Rudolf Steiner Press, 1999.

————. *World Economy,* London: Rudolf Steiner Press, 1977. Also published as *Economics: The World as One Economy,* Bristol, England: New Economy Publications, 1996.

Steiner, Rudolf and Ita Wegman. *Extending Practical Medicine: Fundamental Principles Based on the Science of the Spirit,* London: Rudolf Steiner Press, 1996.

Thoreau, Henry David. "Life Without Principle," in *Thoreau: Walden and Other Writings,* New York: Bantam Books, 1965, pp. 355–359.

Tocqueville, Alexis de. *Democracy in America,* New York: Penguin Books, 1984.

Washington, Booker T. *Up from Slavery,* Pathfinder edition, New York: Bantam Books, 1967.

Zachos, Paul. "Discovering the True Nature of Educational Assessments," *Research Bulletin* (Wilton, NH: The Research Institute for Waldorf Education) vol. 9, no. 2 (2004): pp. 7–12.